15.

THE CZECHS AND SLOVAKS IN CANADA

UNIVERSITY OF TORONTO PRESS

THE CZECHS

AND SLOVAKS

IN CANADA

JOHN GELLNER AND JOHN SMEREK

SBN 8020 1511 5

Published on the occasion of the Centennial of Canadian Confederation.
The preparation of the manuscript was subsidized by
the Centennial Commission.

Ouvrage publié à l'occasion du Centenaire
de la Confédération Canadienne,
et rédigé grâce à une subvention de la Commission du Centenaire.

Published in association with
MASARYK MEMORIAL INSTITUTE

Preface

Since this book is a first attempt at tackling its subject, we were without any established guidelines or precedents, but we were thus free to choose the general scope and direction to be taken in the following pages. It would have been just possible for us to have told two separate histories, but we chose—and, as we shall see, more appropriately—to deal jointly with the history of the Czechs and Slovaks in Canada as constituting a single theme.

The terms "nation," "nationality," "ethnic group," are vague enough to be variously defined, narrowly if the occasion demands, broadly at other times and in other places. If we have taken the wider view and see the Czechs and Slovaks as one entity, a single group composed of two closely connected but still distinct Slavic units, we think we are on entirely firm ground.

First of all, although the two languages are different, they are uncommonly close to one another: a Czech understands Slovak without difficulty, and a Slovak Czech. There is never any need for translation. A good many publications are written partly in Czech, partly in Slovak. In fact, there are perhaps no other two languages as separate yet as tightly allied as are Czech and Slovak. There are certainly none among the Romance or Germanic tongues; among the Slavic, Serb and Croat form perhaps a comparable couple, but

Russian and Ukrainian, for example, are already farther apart. In any case, the Czech and Slovak languages have a geographic tendency to melt into one another. Where they touch, in the Moravian-Slovakian borderland, there is a local idiom which is a fusion of the two. There, it largely depends on one's education and later career whether one becomes Czech or Slovak. The first president of Czechoslovakia, Thomas Garrigue Masaryk, is perhaps the best example of this. Describing his youth in the fifties of the last century, he once remarked: "I was really half Slovak from my early years. My father was a Slovak from Kopčany who spoke Slovak until his death, and I, too, spoke a tongue more akin to Slovak. I certainly was not cognizant that there was any difference between the Slovaks of Hungary and those of Moravia among whom I grew up." Still, Masaryk was generally counted a Czech, because, living in the Czech environment, he later spoke and wrote in Czech. From that same area where the two languages intermingle have come writers equally proficient in Czech and Slovak. A contemporary example, much discussed of late, is the novelist and essayist, Ladislas Mňačko.

The similarity of literary Czech and Slovak could perhaps in part be explained by the fact that, right into the nineteenth century, Czech was the liturgical language of the Slovak Protestants; and since they were producing most of the writings in the vernacular, Czech became in a way the literary language. As we explain in our first chapter, the Slovak intellectuals decided to change this in the forties of the last century, and for very good reasons. It is significant, though, that they made it decisively clear that they did not intend this step to lead to division. Said their leader, L'udovit Štúr: "God preserve us from being torn away from the Czechs. Who will part now from his brothers must take upon himself a heavy load of responsibility before his nation. We want to retain our bond with them in the future just as we have before; we want to make our own whatever excellence they produce, keep our spiritual relationship, do for them all the good we can, just as we expect this in return from them as our brothers." The comparative newness of the present Slovak literary language does not, however, provide a full explanation for the similarity of Czech and Slovak. The spoken languages are, as we already said, and always have been quite similar.

What has divided the Czechs and the Slovaks into the two distinct ethnic units they are today is their history. In Chapter One we tell briefly how it came about that for over one thousand years the Czechs and the Slovaks had to go their separate political ways. Throughout the centuries, it was more difficult for the Slovaks to retain their identity, but they did. And, almost miraculously, they also managed to cling to their contact, their relationship, with the Czechs. There is no denying that it was they who did most for Czecho-Slovak spiritual unity on the occasions when the Czechs tended to forget that they had blood-brothers on the other side of the Little Carpathians.

The Czechoslovak liberation movement of the First World War sealed the bond which had existed throughout the centuries. It produced the idea of unity which found its political expression in the new Czechoslovak Republic. At its founding, in 1918, there were hardly any Czechs or Slovaks who would have contended that these two ethnic units did not form one entity, one larger national group.

It could perhaps have been expected that the realization of a centuries-old dream, one accompanied by a good measure of romantic notions, would be followed by some disenchantment as the Czechs and Slovaks met the reality of common responsibilities and shared practical problems. The disparate historical development of the two groups was bound to make itself felt eventually. Still, the resulting difficulties were minor compared to the impressive social and economic achievements of Czechoslovakia; before Munich they did not seriously affect the political stability of the country. But they did lead to the growth of a Slovak separatist movement of a kind which simply had not existed in 1918, but which was nevertheless always a minority movement, as the results achieved by Hlinka's Slovak People's party in successive democratic elections proved. Still, once Hitler had decided on the total destruction of Czechoslovakia and as one of the means to this end had thrown his support behind the Slovak separatists, the latter prevailed. The autocratic, one-party Slovak State was established in 1939. And though it was short-lived, collapsing with Nazi Germany in 1945, it left behind a heritage of separatist, and thus implicitly anti-Czech, tendencies.

It is, of course, impossible, under present political conditions, to test the strength of Slovak separatism in present-day Czechoslovakia. All indications are, however, that it is utterly negligible, scarcely deserving to be called a political force at all. Where popular opinion does come into the open in spontaneous fashion, as for instance in the recent strong demand of the Czechoslovak writers for intellectual freedom, it is invariably a Czech *and* Slovak manifestation. If there are any distinctions, they are in accent rather than substance. All in all, it would appear that the common hardships and bitter disappointments of the post-war years have resulted in a further strengthening of the fraternal bonds linking Czechs and Slovaks.

On the other hand, separatism is certainly significant among the Slovaks in North America. This is understandable since a high proportion of the leading supporters of the defunct Slovak State fled to this continent. They represented the first massive influx of intellectuals into the older immigrant group, and, accordingly, they have been able to exercise considerable influence. These alumni of the Slovak State contribute substantially to keeping alive the idea of Slovak separateness, at any rate abroad.

In the Slovak community in Canada there are also a good number of separatists. Naturally, no vote to determine how many there are was ever taken nor could be. We are certain, however, that the great majority of Slovak Canadians feel themselves ethnically linked with the Czechs, and that every new Slovak immigrant, from among the few who nowadays can come from Czechoslovakia, adds to their number. We see Slovak separatism as an aberration of the past, excusable perhaps under the circumstances of the day, but otherwise the sooner forgotten the better. We also believe that the Canadian government was absolutely right in classifying, consistently, from 1918, onwards, Czech and Slovak immigrants in a single category. There was never any point in acknowledging what proved to be only a passing historical phase.

Even so, we have felt it necessary to explain in this Introduction the more fundamental reasons for treating as one the history of the

Czechs and Slovaks in Canada. This is apart from the more immediate and indeed compelling reason that in this country the destinies of these two ethnic units have been intertwined from the earliest days of immigration, and that it thus would be impossible to deal adequately (or for that matter, intelligibly) with their histories in separation. The authors of this book would certainly have found it impossible to do so, although one of them is a Czech, a graduate of a Czech university, who speaks Czech and no Slovak; and the other a Slovak, a graduate of a Slovak university, who speaks Slovak and no Czech.

Another problem, this one arising from the absence of any earlier systematic work in the field, was to give to this book a firm orientation. We decided to hold to the sole task of describing the development and present condition of the national group, without deviation into other areas, however inviting. Consequently, we have dealt only with those organizations which we believe have influenced the development of the Czechs and Slovaks in this country, and with personalities who, we consider, have furthered that development or who at least appear to us to be characteristic of the national group and its aspirations. We consciously avoided making the book either a listing of all Czech and Slovak activities in this country or a Czech and Slovak *Who's Who*. Readers who may wonder why this or that event, or this or that personality, is not mentioned should bear this criterion in mind.

Still, there are no doubt omissions, regrettable but unavoidable. It must be remembered, though, that we worked largely on untrodden land and to a very large extent had to use primary sources. Although we got much help from many quarters, for which we are deeply thankful, there were also a number of occasions when co-operation was promised more readily than subsequently given. Much digging preceded any real finds, and these were few enough. Nevertheless, even if this book turns out to be only a basis for further work—and we flatter ourselves that it is more than that—it will have achieved much of its purpose.

We would assure any who may feel that we have omitted matters of substance that we have tried always to be completely objective.

We can, perhaps, only hope to have succeeded in this; and where we may not have, it was certainly not for lack of good will. All that we say can be taken at face value; there are no hidden motives. For instance, if we consistently speak of the Czechs and Slovaks in this order, it is not because we would put the ones before the others or that we do not recognize that there are more Slovak-Canadians than Czech-Canadians, but simply because the two ethnic units are commonly referred to in this manner, as in the word "Czechoslovakia." Neither in this instance, nor in any others, should judgments be imputed to us which we do not make frankly in the text.

The assistance of the Centennial Commission and the Masaryk Memorial Institute have been acknowledged in earlier pages of this work. Both gave monetary grants for the research and the eventual writing of the book, and the Masaryk Memorial Institute also took an active interest in its publication. Messrs. Charles Cvachovec, Rudolph Fraštacký, and Prokop Havlík made up an informal committee which gave valuable advice at various stages of the project.

Those who gave us important information orally are too many to be listed here. With no earlier work in this field, we were particularly dependent on the individual people, who readily shared their memories with us. We would like to express our heartfelt gratitude to them all. Some of them are mentioned in the text of the book, and of the others, we would like to acknowledge the help given us by Reverends D. Jurkovič, G. Janda, J. Novák; by Drs. Nadežda Hradsky-Ivanková, Bohuslav Dérer, Frank Orlický; and by Messrs. Michael Ferik, Henry Zoder, Mike Janeček, Rudolph Šušanik, George Hlubuček, George Pokorný, Oscar Morawetz, John Mráček, George Corn, Anthony Daičar, and Ervín Sypták. Staff members of the Toronto Public Library have been of great assistance, especially in our research into the work of the Moravian Brethren in Upper Canada and Labrador.

J.G. & J.S.

Toronto April 1968

Contents

THE CZECHS AND SLOVAKS IN CANADA

CHAPTER ONE

Eleven hundred years of recorded history

The general history of the brother nations of Czechs and Slovaks, long and highly interesting though it is, pertains to our subject only as a background which must be sketched in (or recalled) if the nature of the Czech and Slovak immigration into Canada and the characteristics of the Czech and Slovak immigrants are to be properly understood. This background serves also to reveal the origins of the ties which have always existed between the Czechs and Slovaks and which continue here in Canada.

The reader should remember this is only a sketch: one cannot do more in one chapter with some eleven hundred years of recorded history. The well-informed reader may consider our presentation cavalier and over-simple, but he might bear in mind the purpose of this chapter and perhaps forgive us for not allowing this or that part in the rich history of the Czechs and Slovaks the treatment it may deserve.

CHRISTIANITY AND THE
GREAT MORAVIAN EMPIRE

When they entered east-central Europe, the Czechs and Slovaks belonged to what has been called the Northwest group of Slavic tribes. This group had begun to move westwards sometime in the first century AD, and included also the Poles and a number of clans such as the Wends and Lužice Serbs which, venturing west of the Oder river, later merged with the Germanic peoples.

Most of the Czechs and Slovaks—there was undoubtedly no such differentiation between them at that time, and we are using these terms only for convenience—and a great part of the other Northwest Slavs, were united at the end of the eighth century under one ruler, Mojmír I. His domain and that of his successors is referred to as the Great Moravian State or the Great Moravian Empire, at one time it extended from the river Saale, in what is now East Germany, to the Danube. This first—and last, if one discounts two relatively short later interludes—unification of the Northwest Slavs was the direct consequence of the final defeat of the Avars by Charlemagne's son Pippin, king of Italy, in 796. He seems to have been helped by the "king" of Moravia, who thereupon proceeded to carve out what was for those days a veritable empire from the territories in which the Avars had maintained a more or less effective overlordship.

The Great Moravian State lasted only a little over a hundred years. The eastern portion (Slovakia) was eventually conquered by the Magyars; the western (Bohemia and Moravia) became a clearly defined political entity under a domestic dynasty, the Přemyslides. (The outlying domains of the Great Moravian State similarly acquired separate identities—Poland, for instance, under the later dynasty of the Piasts.) Without claiming complete historical exactitude, we can accept the year 896, considered by the Magyars as the year their state was founded, as the fateful date on which the Czechs were politically divided from the Slovaks. Henceforth, the two brother nations developed on separate lines materially, but on parallel lines spiritually.

During the era of the Great Moravian State occurred an event of the utmost importance, both in itself and in the way it happened: the conversion to Christianity of the Czechs and Slovaks. The Middle Ages have justly been called "an epoch which was dominated by the spirit of otherworldliness, and accordingly ruled by the clerical power which represented the other world." Had the Great Moravian State survived, this clerico-political power would likely have been exercised from the east—with far-reaching consequences, the most important of which would have been that the Northwest Slavs would not have lost contact, as they eventually did, with their eastern and southern brethren.

Christianity first came to the Czech and Slovak lands in the early ninth century. Quite recent archaeological finds in the Morava River basin leave us uncertain as to the precise date and location of the first Christian community in these lands. It will be safer therefore to stick to the "established" theory according to which the first Christian church in the regions occupied by the Western Slavs was at Nitra, in present-day Central Slovakia, and was consecrated by Archbishop Adalram of Salzburg in either 833 or 835 AD. This foundation occurred under the rule of Prince Pribina of Nitra, who at the time was not yet a Christian (he was baptised later, in exile) but who nevertheless seems to have been sympathetic to the new faith. Soon afterwards, Pribina's domain was absorbed by Mojmir's spreading Great Moravian Empire.

At any rate, Christianity made its real impact on the Czechs and Slovaks only with the arrival of eastern missionaries, the Slav Apostles Cyril and Method who came from Salonica. It was clearly for political reasons that Rostislav of Moravia asked Emperor Michael of Byzantium and not the Carolingian emperor, Louis the German, to send Christian missionaries. There was no pressure upon Rostislav's realm from the south-east, but a good deal of it from the west. He was not eager to increase it by bringing in German clerics.

Rostislav was converted by the Slav Apostles in 863, and the Přemyslide Bořivoj of Bohemia by Method—Cyril having died in 869 —about the year 880. The liturgy was in the vernacular, a kind of Slavic *lingua franca*, written in a distinctive (Cyrillic) script. Great religious centres arose in Nitra, in Slovakia, and on the Velehrad in Moravia. Method himself became the first archbishop of the Northwest Slavs, his seat being at Sirmium in Pannonia, on the Sáva river. Unfortunately, the unifying influence of the Slavonic rite, which had provided the Great Moravian State in its best years with much of its tensile strength, did not last beyond Method's death (885). His successor, Gorazd, by all indications a local man, was expelled, together with all the priests of the Slavonic rite, and the Latin liturgy brought in from Germany. Those dismembered limbs of the Great Moravian State which after the latter's fall managed to cling to their independence came under the jurisdiction of the German archbishoprics of Salzburg, Regensburg, and Mainz.

However great the spiritual benefits it brought, politically, the victory of Latin-rite Christianity in the lands of the Czechs and Slovaks caused undeniable difficulties. One need not be an advocate of pan-Slavism (a movement largely associated with Orthodoxy) to state this. Yet, in one way, the Slovaks at least benefited from that victory. Latin remained the common, neutral, official language of the multi-national Hungarian kingdom right into the nineteenth century, thus deferring Magyarization and giving the Slovaks the necessary respite to survive the later onslaught of Magyar nationalism.

THE CZECHS
UNDER THE PŘEMYSLIDES

With the incorporation of the last of the Slovak lands into the Hungarian counties (*comitates*) system in 1027 by the Arpád king, Stephen I (St. Stephen), the Slovaks disappeared from the pages of world political history for something like eight hundred years. The pendulum swings to the Czechs who just about that time were entering a great, and sometimes glorious, five centuries in their national life.

If the Czechs are wont to speak of the Germans as the "enemy from time immemorial," they state a fact firmly founded in history. The Czech Carthage finally fell in 1620, after it had battled the German Rome, with varying fortunes, for many centuries. This life-and-death struggle left marks on the Czech nation which would be clearly discernible today even if they had not been burnt in more deeply by the recent Hitlerite aggression. The anti-Germanism of the Czechs is a political factor which perhaps tends to distinguish Czechs from Slovaks; the latter have not had the same experience, at least not to anything like the same degree. Nor is the Slovak antagonism towards the Magyars a comparable attitude, for it is much later in date and thus less of an hereditary attitude.

"The German fact" lies at the core of Czech history. It was already so under the Přemyslides. At first, with the Magyar danger paramount in the European mind, the dukes of Bohemia were prepared to be real allies rather than just nominal liegemen of the German emperors; and with this the latter were by and large content. When Emperor Otto I finally defeated the Magyars on the Lechfeld in 955, he did so with important help from Boleslav I of Bohemia (who had slain his brother, "Good King" Wenceslas). Lechfeld, incidentally, was one of those turning points of European history, like the defeat of Attila the Hun on the Catalaunian Fields in 451, and the providential lifting of the Tartar siege of Olomouc in 1241.

During the eleventh and twelfth centuries, the Přemyslide rulers of Bohemia continued to get along with the generally strong German emperors. Twice in their struggles with the papacy, the emperors received strong support from Bohemia. Vratislav II stood loyally by Henry IV, whom Pope Gregory VII brought to heel at Canossa in 1077, and was made king for life in return. (He was the first true king of Bohemia; St. Wenceslas was so in legend only.) Then, almost a century later, Vladislav II again supported the Hohenstaufen emperor, Frederick Barbarossa, and was rewarded with the hereditary kingship. At the same time, gradually, and often contrary to the policies of the Czech rulers, the links which bound Bohemia to the German-Roman Empire tightened. The duke, and later the king, of Bohemia was one of the seven electors of the Holy Roman Empire, whose head held the rights of ratifying the succession to the Bohemian throne and of appointing the bishop of Prague.

It was also in the declining years of the twelfth century that large-scale German colonization began almost simultaneously in the Czech and Slovak lands. By the middle of the thirteenth century it had turned into a flood. In Upper Hungary, the Slovak part of the kingdom, the German burghers of the "twenty-four towns" of the Spiš gained a good measure of self-government, with even a capital, Levoča. So did the "king's German guests" in Košice, and their compatriots in the mining towns of Banská Bystrica, Zvolen, Štiavnica, and Kremnica. In the Czech lands, German colonists also settled in rural areas, but in the Slovak lands they did this only quite exceptionally. They flowed, of course, in great numbers into the towns, where they were soon given charters allowing them to govern themselves in accordance with German city law. Here lie the origins of the "Sudetenland," which gained such baleful prominence some seven hundred years later. Here, too, is the basis for the principal objection the Sudeten Germans raised against their expulsion from Czechoslovakia after the Second World War: whatever their collective guilt during the Hitler period, after more than seven centuries of settlement, they claimed the rights of autochthons.

The house of the Přemyslides attained its highest flowering towards the end of the dynasty, with the 27th, 28th, and 29th rulers of a line of 31, who in five centuries of uninterrupted reign gave Bohemia the most stable government of all European countries. These kings, Otakar I, Wenceslas I, and Otakar II, energetically pursued the building of an empire entirely independent of Germany. So successful were they that in the Golden Bull of 1212 the German emperor renounced his last real rights of suzerainty over Bohemia. Wenceslas I, and especially Otakar II, extended their domains southward and northward, until by 1269 they stretched in a solid belt from the Baltic to the Adriatic. Alas, the Přemyslide dream of greatness did not last for long. In 1273, Rudolf of Habsburg became German emperor. With Hungary as ally, he proceeded to cut the new Bohemian empire down to size. Compelled at first to yield, and to surrender all his possessions except his patrimony of Bohemia and Moravia, Otakar II later decided to stand up and fight. Characteristically, he applied to the fellow Slavic kingdom of Poland to help him oppose "the insatiable lusts of the Germans," and got a rebuff. (Six hundred and sixty years later, in not too dissimilar circumstances, a Czechoslovak president made the same plea, with the same result.) Fighting alone, Otakar II was defeated and killed in the battle of Dürnkrut in 1278, and Bohemia/Moravia reverted to being a fief of the empire. Twenty-eight years later, the great Přemyslide dynasty died out in the male line with Otakar II's grandson, Wenceslas III.

THE LUXEMBURGS:
THE CZECHS ON TOP OF THE WORLD

It is at this point, in 1306, that the Habsburgs for the first time enter domestic Czech history, albeit only fleetingly. Claiming his rather dubious rights of suzerainty, Albert I, son of Rudolf of Habsburg and (uncrowned) German-Roman emperor, appointed his son, Rudolf III, as king of Bohemia. To strengthen his claim, he married him to Elisabeth, the widow of the penultimate Přemyslide king, Wenceslas II. But when Rudolf died the following year, the emperor's attempt to put his second son, Frederick, on the Bohemian throne failed. The Habsburgs had appeared on the Czech political horizon as a flickering shaft of lightning presaging the storm that was to come.

In the meantime, the Czech lands acquired a ruling house which for a time surpassed the best of the Přemyslides. They were the Luxemburgs. King John, young son of the German-Roman emperor, Henry VII, ascended the Bohemian throne in 1310 and married—again for reasons of dynastic legitimacy—Elisabeth, sister of the last Přemyslide, Wenceslas III. King John was a rather engaging person, a royal knight-errant who fought on his own account not just at the head of Czech armies but in any war in which he could join. He had prayed God that there might be no battle without the Czech king present, and his great wish was abundantly fulfilled. In 1346, by which time he had become blind, he fell at the battle of Crécy fighting for the king of France against the English. Although he was hardly ever in Prague and did as good as nothing for his own realm, he incidentally acquired Silesia, thus rounding out the traditional Czech lands or "lands of the Crown of St. Wenceslas"—of Bohemia, Moravia, and Silesia.

His son and successor Charles (Charles IV as the German-Roman emperor he later became) was a man of very different calibre. When he took over his patrimony in 1346, he found it neglected and impoverished, and Prague itself desolate; he left it a city of splendour, and the Czech lands the heart of Europe. He spoke Czech fluently, and differed from his father and most princes of his generation in that he was not a warrior but a diplomat and a well-educated and studious man. This he showed when he founded Prague University, in 1348, the first such seat of learning in central Europe, and in its impact on the age almost at once the equal of the three great universities of Bologna, Paris, and Oxford. Its international character was reflected in its manner of self-administration, conducted through four "nations," only one of which contained the native Czechs (and with them also the Hungarians and southern Slavs). That the Czechs were greatly outnumbered at the university by foreign masters and students, in particular Germans, became a matter of great import two generations later, in the times of John Hus.

Many of Charles' works still stand: St. Vitus Cathedral, for instance, and Charles' Bridge, built for eternity, which carries automobile traffic now as it did horse-drawn 620 years ago. There is much evidence that Charles, who was really French, if not by race then certainly by upbringing, later harboured sentiments which now we might call Slavic nationalism. For example, he founded the Benedictine monastery of Emauzy, under the Slavonic rite, with imported Croat monks three hundred years after the Great Schism—the breach between the eastern and western Christian churches—had become final. Lest it be thought that Charles was politically motivated by a desire for an accommodation between Rome and Byzantium, it must be remembered that he openly showed his devotion to the memory of the Slav Apostles, Cyril and Method, although they had been variously suspected of Arian heresy. (They were, in fact, only canonized in 1881, almost a thousand years after Method's death.) At any rate, it is certain that Charles was always Czech king first, and German-Roman emperor second.

This greatest of the Czech kings, whose reign has been called the "Golden Age of Bohemia," died in 1378 and was succeeded by his son, the king-emperor, Wenceslas IV. With him we enter the Hussite period. As Hussitism left an imprint on the Czech nation so deep and lasting that it is still felt today and even had, as we shall see, a certain delayed impact on North America, we must look at this religious-national movement more closely.

THE CZECH REFORMATION

Wenceslas ascended the throne just when the crisis of the papacy was reaching its climax. Despite the progressive secularization of society, the popes had, until the end of the thirteenth century, been able to uphold their claim to universal authority over the Christian world. Thereafter they had fallen on evil days, and in 1378 a schism occurred in the Church with the election of two popes, one of whom, Urban VI, occupied St. Peter's throne in Rome while the other, Clement VII, ultimately established himself in Avignon. Both became dependent on secular protectors. The papacy, which in the preceding three-quarters of a century had already lost most of its immense political power, was now losing its moral leadership over western Christianity as well.

The grievous diminution of papal authority, reflected in a general lowering of the prestige of the whole hierarchy, produced two contradictory effects among the lower clergy: on the one hand, it caused disgraceful demoralization shocking to the faithful; on the other, it spawned movements aimed at reform. These sprang up in many countries, and in various forms: there were probably as many zealots shaking their fists as there were scholars gently wagging their fingers at the clerical iniquity they saw surrounding them. The Czechs had men of both kinds, John Milič of Kroměříž, Adalbert Ranků, Matthew of Janov, and even—rare in those days—a learned layman theologian, Thomas of Štítný. They were distinguished by being popular reformers, not only teaching but also writing (which was not at all common, especially in their discipline) in Czech. As the century progressed, all those in the Czech lands who raised their voices against the "Caesarean clergy" and called for a return to the fundamental "sufficiency of Holy Scripture," came in varying degrees under the influence of John Wycliffe, and particularly of Article X of the Wycliffite tenets which declared it at variance with Holy Scripture for the clergy to have worldly possessions.

The foregoing has to be understood if one wants to see John Hus in the right perspective, not as an isolated phenomenon, a charismatic leader who breathed his spirit into the Czech nation, but rather as the crest of a great wave of self-examination and resultant moral regeneration then sweeping society. Hus was the first of the Christian reformers of the era who, however unwillingly, in fact founded a Reformed Church. At the same time, again unintentionally but inevitably, Hus sparked a great national movement which formed the Czech national spirit and produced certain permanent national characteristics. There is no doubt that the typical Czech egalitarianism—an admirable quality far in advance of its time of origin, even if occasionally it has been taken to the extreme—had its origin in the idealism and comradeship of the Hussite Wars.

John Hus' career is too well known to require repeating here. Suffice it to say that by his teachings he came into conflict both with the Germans and with the official church. From the first of these conflicts, waged in the main inside Prague University, he emerged victorious. By the Decree of Kutná Hora of 1409, the position under which the foreigners controlled three national votes against the single one of the "Czech nation" was reversed—even though they outnumbered the Czechs by more like four to one. Hus became rector, and the Germans, led by the deposed rector, Henning von Baltenhagen, walked out of the university. As far as Hus' religious teachings were concerned, they brought him episcopal warnings and finally, in early 1411, excommunication by John XXIII, one of three popes who were then claiming succession to St. Peter's throne. (Upon being deposed by the Council of Constance in 1415, John XXIII was removed from the list of popes; the name of John XXIII could thus properly be assumed by the predecessor of the present Holy Father.) The King and Queen continued, however, to back Hus. Undeterred by the papal ban, Hus redoubled his reformist work, especially when in 1412 John XXIII ordered money raised in European cities, including Prague, by the sale of indulgences for a crusade against a political enemy, Ladislas of Durazzo, king of Naples. Two years later, when the Council of Constance was called to remove the triple schism in the papacy, Hus decided to answer a summons to attend it. He did so, although still under an edict of excommunication, relying on a safe conduct given him by the German-Roman emperor, Sigismund, Wenceslas IV's younger brother. It proved to be the proverbial scrap of paper and Hus was burnt at the stake as a heretic, in Constance, on July 6, 1415.

The gist of Hus' moral and doctrinal teachings, stripped of all subtlety, was five years later incorporated into the Four Articles of Prague of 1420, the fundamental charter of the Hussite faith. Apart from establishing full freedom of preaching the Word of God, the

The clock on the Old City Hall, Prague

Hradčany Castle, Prague

Bojnice Castle

The High Tatras in Slovakia

The High Tatras in winter

Strečno Castle in Slovakia

exclusion of the clergy from temporal activity, and the subjection to the civil authority of those accused of crime against divine law, they contain one major departure from liturgy. Article II states that "the Holy Sacrament of the Body and Blood of Christ under the two kinds of bread and wine, shall be freely dispensed to all Christians who are not shut off by mortal sin." This is the doctrine which gave to the Hussites the common designation of Utraquists (Latin *utraque*, "each of two, both").

King Wenceslas IV died in 1419, a year before the proclamation of the Four Articles of Prague and Sigismund, nominally at least, became king of Bohemia. The first crusade against the Hussites was mounted and crushed at the gates of Prague, on the hill of Vítkov, by the Czech army under John Žižka of Trocnov. Thereafter, the Hussite movement grew progressively more radical, with the Táborites establishing a truly fundamentalist church in a theocratic society, but even their God-oriented communities, inimical to all worldliness, later seemed too lax to the extremist Horebites or "Orphans." In the eleven years after Vítkov, successive crusades were defeated by the Hussites under Žižka and his successor, the warrior-priest Prokop. They even made deep inroads into the neighbouring regions of Germany and Hungary, notably the Slovak parts of the latter. Sigismund was humiliated, an inimical Europe frustrated; the Czechs were at the pinnacle of their military glory. But they were also tired of continuous war. Consequently, the moderates brushed aside the opposition of the extremists and accepted the invitation extended by the Council of Basel to come and seek a reconciliation with the established Church. Agreement was reached after negotiations lasting more than three years, from early 1433 to the summer of 1436. But before 1436 the Hussite moderates had yet to crush the radical Táborite opposition in the battle of Lípany in 1434, the Hussite general John Bořek of Miletínek achieving what all the crusader armies of Europe had failed to achieve—the defeat of Prokop and his redoubtable followers. The Basel Compacts of 1436 then made the Czech military victory into a political and moral one as well: they were, in substance, a restatement of the Four Articles of Prague.

Hussitism and the Hussite Wars were a great triumph, moral as well as physical, of a small people over a world of enemies. For almost two centuries thereafter, the kingdom of Bohemia occupied a special position in Christendom. Recognized by the Council of Basel (though not formally by the Pope) as "true Christians and genuine sons of the Church," the Czech Utraquists followed a modified liturgy and were spiritually guided by a reformed clergy living in saintly poverty—and matrimonial bonds. For the first time, and the last for hundreds of years, the principle of tolerance had been forced upon the Church.

Yet it was a Pyrrhic victory. The Czech nation became isolated, the object of latent suspicion and ever-smouldering hatred. The Habsburgs, under whose rule the Czechs were destined to come, were always suspicious of a people whom they came to regard as perennial revolutionaries. It has been suggested that it was this ingrained prejudice against the Czechs, formed by the Hussite experience, which as late as the nineteenth and early twentieth centuries inhibited Habsburg policies, so that they missed opportunities of using the Czechs as the backbone of a transformed, modern Austria. This is hard to believe, but not impossible: irrational distrust as a motivating force in history is anything but uncommon. Worst of all, the Czech nation had expended too much of its substance, had exhausted itself physically and spiritually. Lípany was in fact already a manifestation of that exhaustion. From the day of that fratricidal battle the descent from the national apogee began.

THE AFTERMATH
OF THE HUSSITE WARS

The Luxemburgs had come into Czech history with a roar; they went out in a whimper. Sigismund, who had fought his Czech subjects for a disastrous seventeen years, died barely a year after he had finally made it to Prague. He left one daughter, Elisabeth, married to Albert II of Austria. Albert thus succeeded to the thrones of Bohemia and Hungary, inaugurating in 1437 the Habsburg era for the Czechs and Slovaks. Apart from relatively short interruptions, it lasted for almost five hundred years.

Some months after Albert's premature death in 1439, a son was born to Elisabeth, known as Ladislas Posthumus. At different times, various governors ruled for the boy in the several parts of his far-flung domains: John Hunyady in Lower Hungary, George of Poděbrady in Bohemia, and a Czech noble, John Jiskra of Brandýs, in Upper Hungary, the Slovak portion. The Jiskra interlude in Upper Hungary lasted for twenty-two years, from 1440 to 1462, for the Czech *condottiere* held on for another five years after the death of his master, Ladislas Posthumus. It is of considerable interest, for it brought Czechs and Slovaks into close contact at a point in history when the two nations had become largely estranged. Hussitism never took roots among the Slovaks, mainly because they remained unaffected by the Hussite ethos which gave the movement its peculiar strength. And what they saw of the Hussites during the latter's periodic invasions of Upper Hungary, must, if anything, have repelled them. Jiskra's rule amounted to a military dictatorship, based on an army, the core of which was Hussite. Official correspondence was largely conducted in Czech, or in a combination of Czech and Slovak. Slovaks served in the administration and the army. Understandably, considering his background, Jiskra had no love for the Germans; he thus furthered the Slovakization of the predominantly German towns of Upper Hungary. All in all, Jiskra does not seem to have considered himself, or acted as, a foreign occupier, but to have felt perfectly at home as a feudal overlord among the Slovaks, upon whom he looked no differently than on the people around his own estates in western Moravia. If his efficient but turbulent governorship left any lasting mark on the Slovaks, it was a taste for the military life, and with it added national self-confidence.

Jiskra had a Slovak counterpart—"counter" has to be taken literally in this case—in Pongrác of Svätý Mikuláš, a noble who for years ruled over large parts of western and north-western Slovakia. But by 1462, Hungary was united again under the strong hand of Hunyady's son, King Matthias Corvinus, in whose services John Jiskra of Brandýs died on a mission to Constantinople.

In the meantime in Bohemia, George of Poděbrady, after having been regent on behalf of the boy-king for thirteen years, was elected king of Bohemia in 1458 on the death of Ladislas. He was an able ruler, both a warrior and superb diplomat. And he certainly needed all his faculties to uphold his position which was at all times precarious. Despite the Compacts of Basel, he and the majority of his people were generally looked upon as heretics. Even inside his realm, he maintained only with difficulty the fine balance between Utraquists and Catholics. The emperor, Frederick III of Habsburg, and King Matthias Corvinus of Hungary, both recipients of George's aid at one time, made common cause against him. Instead of concentrating on defending the badly threatened eastern and southern frontiers of Hungary against the onrushing Turks, Matthias chose to lead yet another crusade against the heretical Czechs. It was again decisively defeated. Yet King George realized that, although he had been able to maintain himself against all enemies, there was no chance of founding a Poděbrady dynasty. So, before his death in 1471, he arranged for the Diet to offer the crown to the Jagiellon prince, Vladislav, son of Casimir III of Poland.

George was the last king of Bohemia who was a native Czech, and who spoke exclusively Czech. Into his reign falls an event of great significance: the founding of the fundamentalist Christian community of the Unity of the Brethren, Unitas Fratrum, by Brother Gregory, in 1459. Its followers, commonly referred to as the Czech Brethren, became better known abroad as the Moravians, under which name they entered Canadian history. Essentially their aim was a simple Christian life and a return to the faith of apostolic days. They based their lives on the word of the Bible. Practising the concept of the priesthood of all believers, the Unity of Brethren became one of the world's great Christian missionary churches.

FROM REFORMATION

TO COUNTER-REFORMATION

We shall now pass over the period of the Jagiellon kings of Bohemia and Hungary (1471–1526 in Bohemia, 1490–1526 in Hungary)—a period of little relevance for our purposes. One sad development of that period must, however, be recorded which occurred almost at the same time in both kingdoms and thus simultaneously affected the Czechs and the Slovaks: the virtual enslavement of the peasants. In the Czech lands, the final step toward the reduction of the rural population to serfdom was taken more than a century later, but in Hungary a law of 1514 declared the peasant "the servant of his lord for all time." The Slovaks felt this particularly strongly, because the overwhelming majority of them farmed the land.

Two other developments, momentous in the history of the Czechs and Slovaks and of all Europeans, occurred toward the end of the Jagiellon period, although they achieved their full impact only in the following Habsburg era: the spread of Protestantism, and the advance of the Turks into east-central Europe.

The Lutheran doctrine gained ground more readily in the Slovak than in the Czech lands. This is understandable, for in the kingdom of Bohemia there already was a Reformed communion, that of the Utraquists, legally established under the Compacts of Basel and linked, however awkwardly, with the Catholic Church. (Utraquist priests, for instance, were consecrated by Catholic bishops.) Perhaps even more important, Utraquism had historically developed as a religious *and* a national movement. From the times of John Hus and the Hussite Wars it retained a strong anti-German bias. Consequently, even though Martin Luther acknowledged his link with Hus—in a famed letter to his mentor, George Spalatin, he said: "We are all Hussites without having been conscious of it"—his teachings were received by the Czechs with the reservations shown to everything that came from Germany. Finally, the Unity of Brethren, who were spreading despite persecution, could attract those Czechs seeking a church entirely divorced from Rome.

There were no such obstacles to the spread of Lutheranism in the Slovak lands. The German towns adopted the new creed readily, proclaiming between 1549 and 1558 their own slight variations of the Augsburg Confession: the Confessio Pentapolitana for the five royal cities of northern Upper Hungary, and, the Confessio Montana for the seven mining towns of the central parts. Among the Slovak burghers in the German cities, and among the Slovaks in other towns and on the land (as far as they were not debilitated by serfdom), the new communion found adherents. Finally, many of the big land-owners espoused Lutheranism, and a proportion of these, too, were Slovaks.

The Reformation had one interesting side-effect in the lands of the Crown of St. Stephen: at a time when distinctions according to nationality were not nearly as significant politically as they became three hundred years later, and when the modern concept of national-ism was not yet born, the Reformation drew another sharp line between Magyars and Slovaks. The latter, if they left the Catholic Church, became Lutherans, the Magyars Calvinists. In fact, Calvin-ism in Hungary was always distinguished as "a magyar hit," the Magyar faith.

By the middle of the sixteenth century, the Turks had overrun all except Upper Hungary, with the disputed and fluctuating border running roughly where, almost four hundred years later, the frontier was laid between Czechoslovakia and Hungary. Thus, all of a sudden, royal Hungary became a predominantly Slovak country. Bratislava was now the capital, and for a long time to come the coronation city, of the kingdom of Hungary.

After the death in the battle of Mohács of the last Jagiellon king, Louis II, the Czech Estates elected in 1526 the Habsburg archduke, Ferdinand of Austria, as king of Bohemia, he being married to Louis' sister, Anne. On ascending the throne, he took an oath confirming the Estates in their rights, and proclaiming again the equality of the two confessions, Catholic and Utraquist. Eventually, he also became king of what was left of Hungary, mainly the Slovak lands. Under him and his immediate successors, Bohemia became the core of Habsburg power, and Prague, as it once had been under the Luxemburgs, the seat of the king-emperors. Thus practically, if not formally, it was the capital of the Holy Roman Empire.

The last half of the sixteenth century also saw an association be-tween Czechs and Slovaks which, but for developments that came some 250 years later, could have resulted in national fusion. Again, the basic reason was religious, the particular amalgam being Pro-testantism. In Bohemia, Utraquism was becoming an institution without a content. Its "Establishment"—if we may use this modern term to describe something that occurred four centuries ago—tended towards a return into the Catholic fold. The laity was impressed by the religious fervour and purity of life of the Unity of Brethren, to which, even though it was banned, as much as one-half of the non-Catholic Czechs belonged at the end of the century. Others, as far as they were able to shed their anti-German prejudices, inclined toward Lutheranism. In either case, the national character of Czech religious expression remained a peculiarly important factor. It was strengthened by the translation into Czech of the New Testament in 1565 by John Blahoslav, a Unity Brother. Both it and the Old Testament, in Czech, were published in 1593 as the Králice Bible. Together with the first Czech grammar, also by John Blahoslav, the Good Book was also adopted by the Slovak Lutherans, whose liturgical language Czech thus became. In the nature of things this made it the general literary language of the Slovaks, and created a bond which, bearing fruit in the Czech and Slovak Renaissance, was never broken again.

At the same time, Lutheranism in Upper Hungary grew progressively stronger, to the point where it could be institutionalized. In 1610, an Evangelical synod was called to Žilina by the Palatine George Thurzo, at which the country was divided into three ecclesiastical districts, each under its superintendent. Significantly, and in tune with the greatly changed socio-political conditions in the truncated kingdom of Hungary, all three superintendents were Slovaks: Eliáš Láni, Isaac Abrahamides, and Samuel Melik.

The synod of Žilina was held in the last years of the reign of the king-emperor, Rudolf II. For thirty-six years, from 1576 to 1612, this strange man lived in the Castle of Prague, a virtual recluse. He was highly educated and studious, but a mystic of not altogether balanced mind. Though quite ineffectual as a ruler, he did a good deal for his capital and much of it can still be admired in Prague. In his times, the internal chaos caused by religious differences reached its climax, and the Catholic "backlash" of the Counter-Reformation was beginning to make itself felt.

Because it was not enforced by armed might in a religious war, the Counter-Reformation failed to triumph as completely in the Slovak

lands as it eventually did in the Czech. It was highly successful, none
the less. It came after the Council of Trent had taken much of the
wind out of Protestant sails: the Roman Church had reformed itself,
had above all turned energetically against the material abuses which
had impelled people like Hus, Savonarola, and Luther to take the last
step into open revolt. It had also found a keen weapon in the Jesuit
Order. And in Slovakia, the Counter-Reformation had a leader of true
genius in Archbishop Peter Pázmány.

He was, in fact, the very personification of the Counter-Reformation. Son of Calvinistic parents, he converted to Catholicism, joined
the Jesuits, and was educated in their schools, including one at Brno,
in Moravia. After a brilliantly rapid ascent of the rungs of the hierarchy he became archbishop of Esztergom and primate of Hungary
in 1616. As his episcopal seat was in Turkish hands, he resided in
Trnava, in the Slovak part of the kingdom, where the Jesuits had just
established themselves again after a hiatus of some years. Archbishop
Pázmány made Trnava the base for his drive aimed at regaining
Upper Hungary for the Catholic church. He crowned his work by the
foundation there, in 1635, of a university, the first in the country. (A
much earlier attempt resulting in the establishment, in 1467, of the
Academia Histropolitana in Bratislava, was of short duration.) The
Jesuit university was an important, international seat of learning for
142 years, until, in 1777, it was transferred to the capital of the kingdom of Hungary, Buda.

In the Czech lands, where the oldest of all reformed churches had
existed for a century and a half, the Counter-Reformation at first
progressed with much more difficulty than in the Slovak. The fight
was even formally suspended for a while and the existing stalemate
recognized: in Moravia, by Matthias' (Rudolf II's brother and successor) undertaking in 1608 to allow religious liberty; in Bohemia,
by the Letter of Majesty of 1609, which conceded the same while
granting further rights to the Czech Estates. Still, the Counter-
Reformation was as elemental a force as the Reformation had been
in the two preceding centuries. The decisive showdown could be
delayed, but not avoided.

It came in 1618, over a matter which, however trivial, was in the prevailing atmosphere sufficient to set off the fuse. The royal counsellors, Slavata and Martinic, together with their clerk Fabricius, were unceremoniously flung out of a window of Prague Castle ("The Defenestration"). The Jesuits were expelled. And the Estates, strongly Protestant and led by Count Thurn, assumed the *de facto* conduct of affairs of the kingdom, although nominally Matthias remained king until his death, in March 1619.

After that, the sluice-gates of revolt opened fully. The Estates had no intention of recognizing Rudolf II or Matthias' cousin, Ferdinand of Austria and Hungary (even though they had previously, in 1617, "accepted" him as the future king of Bohemia), for he had already proved himself the sharp sword of the Counter-Reformation. Instead, in the summer of 1619, at a general diet in Prague of the Estates of all the lands of the Crown of St. Wenceslas, Ferdinand was deposed and a Protestant, Frederick V, duke of the Palatinate, was elected king of Bohemia. His wife was Elizabeth Stuart, daughter of King James I of England, and their third son, born in Prague about the time of his father's coronation, that same Prince Rupert who later appears in the early pages of Canadian history. Significantly, Frederick was crowned by the administrator of the Protestant (Utraquist) Consistory and the senior of the Unity of the Brethren. It was thus in its dying moments that the Reformation in Bohemia gained the fulness of victory.

That victory was short-lived, indeed. Ferdinand II, having been elected German-Roman emperor, gathered the forces of the Catholic League for an assault against Bohemia. The league's counterpart in the Empire, the Protestant Union, left Frederick in the lurch. The Czech army was decisively defeated on the White Mountain, just outside the city walls of Prague, on November 8, 1620. There is no doubt that the capital could have been defended, but Frederick was not the man for that. He fled, and all resistance collapsed. Retribution against those whom Ferdinand had good reason to consider rebels was swift, but by no means excessive. Altogether, there were twenty-seven executions—seventeenth-century monarchs were generally more humane, because more civilized, than the upstart political strongmen of the twentieth.

Re-Catholization, on the other hand, was advanced with unbending will and single-minded vigour. True, the Letter of Majesty of 1609 of Rudolf II was only revoked by the Renewed Ordinance of 1627, but by then the Counter-Reformation had already had its full effect on the country, which the forced emigration of the Protestants was quickly turning into a Catholic one. The Ordinance also made Bohemia a hereditary kingdom in the Habsburg dynasty, and stripped the Estates of almost all their powers. The German language was placed on a footing of equality with Czech throughout the country. The lands of the Crown of St. Wenceslas ceased to be governed from Prague. Henceforth they would be ruled from Vienna, where the king-emperor resided, and his policies were executed through the Bohemian Court Chancellery. So complete and crushing was the victory of Habsburg power that the Czechs, who for so long had been at the centre of European events—and indeed had often been their moving force—now disappear as a nation from the political scene for more than two centuries.

Among the Czechs who emigrated in order to preserve their religion were the majority of the Brethren. A strong group, containing most of the leaders, left immediately after the proclamation of the Renewed Ordinance and settled in Leszno, in Poland. In it was John Amos Komenský (Comenius), the great philosopher and encyclopaedist who was above all one of the founders of modern pedagogics. A savant of world renown and in many of his ideas far in advance of his times, he later greatly influenced Czech and Slovak thought when he was rediscovered, as it were, first for the Slovaks by Daniel Lehocký toward the end of the eighteenth century, and years later for the Czechs by Francis Palacký. Some thirty thousand Czech Brethren also took refuge in Upper Hungary, where they found more religious tolerance than in conquered Bohemia. Mingling with the local people, they provided embattled Slovak Protestantism with an infusion of new blood.

Some of the Brethren held out in their homeland, practising their religion clandestinely. This was very difficult, and it seems a miracle that some of them managed to do this even a hundred years after the White Mountain. From among them came the group which the

"Moravian Moses," Christian David, led to Saxony under the protection of Count Zinzendorf. These simple men became the renewers of the Unity of the Brethren, which ever since has been called, albeit only outside the Czech and Slovak lands, the Moravian Church. We will hear about them later on in this book, for they and their successors played a part in early Canadian history.

It is a measure of the success of the Counter-Reformation that by the middle of the seventeenth century, a bare three decades after the battle of the White Mountain, the Czech lands, which at one time were on the point of being totally lost to the Roman Church, were almost entirely Catholic, and the Slovak lands predominantly so. As far as the Czechs were concerned, the Counter-Reformation stifled their national development. Not so in the case of the Slovaks who, if anything, gained in national vigour by the re-Catholization drive which they themselves largely sparked and conducted.

THE CZECH AND SLOVAK

RENAISSANCE

The 170 years from 1620 to about 1790 have been called the "Period of Total Eclipse" of the Czech nation. Politically, their lands were run by bureaucrats directed by the central government in Vienna, on lines of a more or less benevolent absolutism. The classes which had access to education, the landed nobility and the townspeople, were German or Germanized. There was no attraction in—and indeed often no way of—expressing oneself in Czech. Spoken currently only by the serfs, the language was archaic and incomplete, lacking the new words which the progress of civilization had made necessary. Not taught in the schools, not written in books, periodicals, or even simple correspondence, Czech was for a time in danger of becoming a dead language.

The Czech National Rebirth, the first faint stirrings of which became noticeable in the last decade of the eighteenth century, was thus something of a miracle. It was sparked by several influences. One was the humanism and modernity of two enlightened emperors, Joseph II (1780–90) and Leopold II (1790–92). Another was the

French Revolution, and the national spirit it engendered; first in France itself where the national *levée en masse* saved the country from foreign enemies, and later elsewhere, particularly in Germany, where a national reaction against Napoleonic oppression proved vastly more effective than dynastic opposition. Finally, there was romanticism, with its racial mystique. Here, especially Johann Gottfried von Herder and his *Ideas on the Philosophy of the History of Mankind* exercised a powerful influence. Herder has been called "the father of the Slav National Renaissance."

Interesting as the history of the Czech Rebirth is, as an extraordinary example of a nation rising phoenix-like from the ashes, we can only trace it here in the broadest outlines. Its forerunners, however full of national consciousness, still communicated their ideas in German rather than in Czech. Similarly, the first learned bodies, bright stars in the still blackness of the cultural night—the Royal Bohemian Society of Sciences founded in 1784, and the Bohemian Museum Society founded in 1818—long transacted their business in German. Even so, they were the centres of renascent Czech cultural life.

The five pioneers of the Czech National Rebirth were, in chronological order: a Czech philologist, the Catholic priest Joseph Dobrovský (1753–1829); a Czech grammarian, Joseph Jungmann (1773–1847); a Slovak poet, the Protestant divine John Kollár (1793–1852); a Slovak archaeologist, Paul Joseph Šafárik (1795–1861), and a Czech historian, Francis Palacký (1798–1876). The two Slovaks—and it is indicative of the close spiritual relationship of Czechs and Slovaks despite what was by then already eight centuries of political separation that two of the five great architects of the Czech Rebirth were Slovaks—wrote in Czech. These men bequeathed to the nation a rejuvenated and grammatically improved language, capable of expressing every thought from poetic to scientific, and a knowledge of its well-nigh forgotten history. With a language that an educated person could use, and a tradition of which anyone could be proud, they imparted to their long-downtrodden countrymen that sense of identity and mission that culminated in the establishment of an independent national home.

The parallel Slovak Revival was, at any rate in the beginning, complicated by the literary language issue. As was said earlier, sixteenth-century Czech—"the language of the (Králice) Bible"—was the liturgical, and consequently the general literary, language of the Slovak Protestants. The nationally minded Catholics, on the other hand, tended toward a native idiom. They found their champion in F. Anthony Bernolák, who established the western Slovak dialect as a literary language and defined its grammar and orthography. He also compiled a Slovak-Czech-Latin-German-Magyar lexicon, and with some associates founded in 1792 the Slovak Learned Society in Trnava, generally known as the Bernolák Society. To his school belonged another Slovak priest, the canon of Esztergom, George Palkovič, who translated the Bible into Slovak in 1831–32. (This had also been done in 1722 by a Slovak Lutheran, Daniel Krman.)

There were thus, in the early nineteenth century, two distinct orientations in the reviving literary life of the Slovaks: the purely Slovak, and the Czecho-Slovak. (Incidentally, this term already was in fairly general use more than a hundred years before the founding of Czechoslovakia: for instance, at the Bratislava Lutheran Lyceum, at which also Palacký was at one time a student, there was a chair of "Czech-Slovak language and literature.") It is idle to speculate on what would have been the consequences if the Czecho-Slovak trend had prevailed. Certain is that the ultimate general acceptance of a Slovak literary language—though not based on Bernolák's western counties', but on the central Slovak dialect propounded by L'udovít Štúr—enabled the Slovak leaders to mobilize all the inner resources of the nation to ward off the deadly peril of Magyarization. It is doubtful if this would have been possible had the written word been spread in a language which, although understandable to all Slovaks, was still not their own. There was, in fact, little resistance to L'udovít Štúr's reforms. He had begun publishing the *Slovak National News* in the new common idiom in 1845. Two years later, all factions agreed on its general usage.

In the meantime, the Czech and Slovak cause had received an important boost by the abolition of most of the personal bonds of serfdom by Emperor Joseph II, and the restriction and *réglementation* of the remaining economic obligations of the peasants, the so-called "robots." Peasant boys could now as a rule go to school and thereafter leave the landlord's land. They swelled the ranks of the Czechs and Slovaks capable of political action. Thus it was that the two brother nations entered the critical year 1848 with a fair measure of self-confidence, even if it was not quite matched by actual strength.

1848

AND DASHED HOPES

Just as sixty years earlier, the wind of change came from France, where the February Revolution had swept away the monarchy and established the Second Republic. The Czechs reacted at once, putting forth a number of political and social demands, but theirs was a fire that soon burned out. A Slavic congress was convoked in Prague, at which Palacký presided, and the Slovak delegation led by Ľudovit Štúr, Miloslav Hurban, and Michael Miloslav Hodža played a prominent role among some 350 participants from all Slavic nations. Šafárik delivered the opening address. Mainly because of the sober political realism of Štúr and of Charles Havlíček, the Czech politician and writer, Czecho-Slovak co-operation was at its most effective. The nation's imagination had been fired by the oratory that flowed at the congress; the dawn of liberty—it was, alas, a *fata morgana*—was seen on the horizon. On June 12, Whit Monday, there was a rising in Prague; young people mounted the barricades. It was in fact only an incident, not a revolution, and the local Austrian commander, Prince Alfred Windischgrätz, gave it short shrift. The congress dispersed hurriedly. Those of the Czech leaders who were thought to be compromised were hustled off to jail, Havlíček to the fortress of Brixen and to early death. Men like Palacký retained a measure of influence on subsequent developments, but as a nation the Czechs left the turbulent scene of the revolutionary years 1848–49.

Even before the congress, Slovak leaders had met at Hodža's house in Liptovský Sväty Mikuláš and on May 10, 1848, had issued the Demands of the Slovak Nation. They amounted to an assertion of national autonomy. The Magyar revolutionary government of Louis Kossuth, himself a Magyarized Slovak from the Turčiansky Svätý Martin region, took strong repressive action. The newly constituted Slovak National Council, headed by Miloslav Hurban, had to operate from outside the country. It raised a volunteer force with which it entered Slovak territory again near Myjava, on September 19, 1848. There, Štúr proclaimed Slovak independence within the Habsburg state.

It is interesting to note that the Slovak National Council's forces contained a good number of Czechs, one of them being the commander of the little army, Frederick Bloudek. This was not accidental. It had a deeper meaning. Ever since the Law of 1836 had supplanted Latin and made Magyar the universal official language of the kingdom of Hungary and Magyarization had begun with full force, Czech leaders had insisted on the fraternal right and obligation of the Czechs to intervene on the Slovaks' side. Thus, in an exchange of letters with Francis Pulszky (later, Kossuth's secretary), which caused considerable stir when they were published in book form, Count Leo Thun emphasized that the language question in Hungary was not a mere local matter. The Czechs, too, were immediately and deeply involved, for "the national contact with the Slovaks contributes to promoting our own intellectual life. . . . We need them just as much as they need us." This was written in 1843, three-quarters of a century before the Czechs and Slovaks confirmed their need for one another by founding a common state.

The Slovak volunteers fought with varying fortunes until the Hungarian revolution was crushed, in the summer of 1849. In the end, the Slovaks who had actively helped the young emperor, Francis Joseph I, to defeat the most dangerous of the several insurrections in the Habsburg empire, did not receive any more or any less than the Czechs who, though not very energetically, had been insurgents themselves. The proverbial "thanks of the House of Habsburg" left the Slovaks in precisely the same position as before the Myjava proclamation, subjects of a kingdom of Hungary preserved in its pre-revolutionary frontiers.

THE COMPROMISE OF 1867

The wave of revolutions that swept through Europe in 1848 was more than just a quest for full political emancipation. Occurring at a time when the western world was just at the threshold of the industrial age, these revolutions challenged sluggish, reactionary regimes to modernize their creaking governmental machinery to cope with the political, economic, and social problems of the new era. Of all the governments so challenged, the Austrian was the most reluctant to harken to the clarion call of the revolution. Except for its abolition of the "robot," the last iniquitous institution of serfdom, it rejected reform, choosing instead to tighten the screws of absolutism. It is for this above all that Emperor Francis Joseph I must be blamed. At the age of nineteen, he might have been expected to have a more open mind than his two benighted predecessors, feeble-minded Ferdinand I, and, rigid to the point of fossilation, Francis II.

The only lesson the young emperor seems to have learned from the vicissitudes and humiliations through which he had had to go in 1848–49 was that, in politics, it can be useful to roll with the punches: not yield an inch if it is not absolutely necessary, but yield plenty when in danger of being knocked down. Pursuing this policy, a mixture of stubbornness and giving in gracelessly, made him miss many a political opportunity during his sixty-eight years' reign. Perhaps the greatest opportunity he let go by—and here the failure in the end proved fatal to state and dynasty—was giving a structure to his empire that would be acceptable to its many nationalities.

The choice was between absolutist centralism and constitutional federalism. The emperor tried the former for some years, though it was obvious that such form of government could no longer be sustained. In fact, it had been dangerously obsolete for at least a quarter of a century. Prince Metternich, much maligned as an opponent of all progress, realized as far back as 1817 that centralism would have to be supplanted by a system that would take heed of the racial differences in the empire. He consequently recommended its division into six administrative units, one each for the Czechs and Poles, the Germans, the South Slavs (he called them Illyrians), the Italians, the Hungarians, and the various nationalities inhabiting Transylvania. His plan followed provincial not ethnic divisions, and thus left the Slovaks, for instance, still under the proposed Hungarian sub-chancellery. Still, the basic idea was right. Needless to say that with an emperor of Francis II's ilk, it got nowhere.

Federalist plans were urged upon Francis Joseph repeatedly, but, as they were not accompanied by a strong enough punch, to no avail. The one nation he considered capable of punching hard were the Magyars —their revolution, which he had only been able to subdue after he had called in a Russian army, stuck in his mind as a traumatic experience. There were other factors which made Francis Joseph gradually incline toward Austro-Hungarian dualism; they ranged from family influences to heavy pressures imposed by disasters in foreign policy, especially the lost wars of 1859 and 1866. The fact that dualism was a negation of the fundamental idea of the Austrian state—that of a multiracial empire held together by an impartial dynasty belonging to no nation and yet to all—the emperor did not grasp. He was intellectually too limited, even though otherwise he did not lack shrewdness or physical and moral courage.

There was plenty of warning that the other nationalities would reject dualism, and consequently the dualist state, because it gave privileged positions to two among them: the Magyars in the Hungarian part of the empire, the Germans in the Austrian. The Slovaks, for instance, met in strength in Turčiansky Svätý Martin in the summer of 1861. There, with John Francisci as president and Stephen Daxner as draftsman of the final resolutions, they issued a memorandum in which they demanded the recognition of the "individuality of the Slovak nation" and the establishment of a semi-autonomous Slovak region of Upper Hungary. The memorandum of 1861 was submitted to the emperor in December of that year, by a delegation headed by Bishop Stephen Moyses of Banská Bystrica. It was a strong protest against any plan that would force the Slovaks into being second-class citizens in a Magyar state, but it was not a punch with which the emperor would have found it necessary to roll.

Nor were the Czech protests likely to produce that effect. Palacký summarized them in a brilliant series of articles which appeared in

1865 under the title of "The Idea of the Austrian State." For a long time, the eminent historian had firmly believed that the Habsburg state was a socio-political necessity in polyglot east-central Europe. Now, just as clearly, he foresaw that the adoption of the dualistic system must make it a socio-political impossibility. "Domestic peace will turn into conflict," he warned, "hope into desperation, to bring forth first friction and then an all-out fight. . . . We Slavs look forward to such a development with aching hearts, but without fear. We were before Austria was; we will be when it is no longer."

At the eleventh hour, in 1866, Slavic leaders met in Vienna and drew up an alternative plan which would have transformed the empire into a "pentarchy," composed of five national states: a German, a Czech, a Hungarian (including a semi-autonomous Slovak region), a Polish, and a South Slav. It got no further than the one Metternich had submitted half a century earlier, and the several others which had been mooted in between.

The Compromise with Hungary became an accomplished fact in March 1867. In December of that year, the already truncated Austrian parliament, the Reichsrat, in which the Austrian Germans now predominated, gave its inevitable, formal sanction to what was by then an accomplished fact. Henceforth, there were two Habsburg states joined in personal union, the Empire of Austria and the Apostolic Kingdom of Hungary. There were only three joint ministries, those of war, foreign affairs, and finance, but the last of these functioned under an only temporary brief, the economic relationship between the two sovereign states being subject to decennial renegotiation. The Czechs did not fare badly under the comparatively liberal Austrian constitution, which gave fairly wide powers to the provincial diets. The Slovaks, on the other hand, were given over entirely to the small mercies of the centralist Magyar government in Budapest. Once again, and under worse circumstances than ever before, they were left to struggle as best they could for bare national survival.

We felt it necessary to dwell on the Compromise of 1867, even at the peril of going beyond our terms of reference, since that one momentous event underlies all which happened in the half century that ended with the dismemberment of Austria-Hungary and the founding of Czechoslovakia. The Compromise was truly the *finis Austriae*; 1918 was merely the conclusion of an irresistible process of disintegration.

FROM COMPROMISE TO WAR

The Compromise of 1867 removed the last restraints to ruthless Magyarization in the Hungarian part of the Dual Monarchy. At the same time, it had the effect of enhancing the position of the Czechs in the Austrian part, where they were now numerically second only to the Germans, while economically they became in due course the latters' equals. As a result, the development of the two brother nations in the next half century was on completely different lines. The Czechs, politically and otherwise, grew progressively stronger; the Slovaks fought a desperate, and seemingly losing, battle merely to stay alive as a nation. Seton-Watson believes that such was the impact of Magyarization, pushed by all conceivable means fair or foul, that "in another generation, especially if the Central Powers had been victorious [in the First World War] assimilation would have been virtually complete." Whether or not he is right on this point is debatable: Czech and Slovak history shows that nations can find in themselves extraordinary forces of resistance and summon them in time of desperate need. He is undoubtedly correct, however, when he describes the effect the plight of the Slovaks had on the Czechs: "Not the least of the causes of discontent and unrest among the Czechs, while their own movement gained daily in momentum, was the consciousness that their Slovak brethren were in imminent danger of extinction, and that conditions in the Monarchy rendered them impotent to help."

After a period of complete, stern refusal to co-operate in the government of post-Compromise Austria, the Czechs relented when Count Edward Taafe became prime minister in 1879 and began his fourteen years' regime with language decrees that offered justice to the non-German nationalities of Austria. The division into two parts, one Czech and one German, of the ancient Charles University of Prague, which had been in German hands since the Counter-Reformation, finally gave to the Czechs a seat of higher learning. A great number of Czech secondary schools were opened. Officials were enjoined to at least try to deal with parties in their native tongue.

All these concessions were strenuously opposed by the Austrian Germans. A kind of political and social guerilla warfare developed between the latter and the Czechs, at all levels, from the Reichsrat down to the local cultural associations. When the prime minister, Count Casimir Badeni, issued his Language Ordinance of 1897, which would have given complete equality in the Czech lands to the Czech and German tongues (the principal provisions were that every case before a court or government bureau was to be dealt with in the language of the first submission, and that officials appointed after July 1, 1901, were to be bilingual) the Germans succeeded in forcing the government to withdraw the regulation. By and large, it can be said that the central government in Vienna tried to be as fair as the vagaries of the political situation permitted it to be. Still, from time to time it did take repressive measures against the Czechs. In 1893, for instance, there was the so-called Omladina Trial in which members of the university were prosecuted and sentenced for high treason, and it was followed by a long period of martial law in Prague. Martial law was again imposed, for a shorter time, in 1908.

Even so, the Czechs made progress, slowly but irresistibly, in their drive toward full equality. They were helped by the comparative liberality of successive Austrian governments, shown by the introduction of universal male suffrage at the end of 1906, and by the fact that the Emperor had no particular reason to favour Austrian Germans who were looking more and more across the border to Germany. In any event, the German hegemony in the Reichsrat was broken by the electoral reform law, which made representation in parliament proportionate to the numerical strength of the nationalities.

There was, thus, a flickering hope that despite the iniquity of the compromise of 1867 and the smouldering anger of the Czechs and Austrian South Slavs at the treatment their brethren were getting in Hungary, the struggle of the nationalities in the Austrian part of the Dual Monarchy might be composed. What hope there may have been was, however, dashed in 1914 when the emperor's government, insensitive to the feelings of the Slavic majority in the country, recklessly embroiled itself in war with Austria-Hungary's Slavic neighbours, Russia and Serbia.

In the meantime, the government in Budapest had taken a series of important steps aimed at completely Magyarizing the non-Magyar nationalities in the Hungarian part of the Dual Monarchy. In 1874, Prime Minister Koloman Tisza (who had once brushed aside a protest with the blunt statement, "There is no Slovak nation") closed the Slovak secondary schools. One year later, he suppressed the Slovenská Matica, the principal cultural organization of the Slovaks. A later prime minister, Baron Dezider Bánffy, decreed in 1898 that all state officials must Magyarize their names. This produced the so-called "one-crown Magyars," the modest sum of one crown, about twenty-five cents at the then rate of exchange, being all that was required to comply with the noble Baron's command. Finally, in 1907, the minister of education, Count Albert Apponyi, a man who had the reputation of being liberal-minded, ordered the closure of even the private non-Magyar schools. Henceforth, Slovak children could no longer get their education in their mother tongue. It can be well imagined what would have happened to the Slovak nation had this state of affairs endured not, as it eventually did, for another eleven years, but for one or two generations.

Politically, too, the Slovaks were as good as disfranchised. Whereas in the Austrian part of the Dual Monarchy universal male suffrage gave to the Czechs in the lands of the Crown of St. Wenceslas the majority representation to which they were entitled in view of their numbers, in Hungary, restrictive electoral laws, gerrymandering, and the occasional outright electoral fraud virtually deprived the Slovaks who wanted to remain Slovaks of any influence on the affairs of the state. In the elections of 1906, for instance, only three Slovaks got into the Budapest parliament when by their numbers they should have been entitled to at least ten times that number. (One of the three was Dr. Milan Hodža, who later played a leading role in Czechoslovak politics.) The severe and archaic restrictions in the franchise, of course, hurt the poorer Magyars as well, but they at least were, however indirectly and ineffectively, represented by the deputies from the Magyar privileged classes.

Deprived of institutes of higher learning, young Slovaks went to study at the Czech university in Prague. There many of them came under the influence of a brilliant professor of philosophy who, about the turn of the century, at the age of fifty, was beginning to make his mark in Czech politics, Thomas Garrigue Masaryk. Some of his Slovak disciples, led by Dr. Vavro Šrobár, Dr. Paul Blaho, and Anthony Štefánek, returned home to found the revue *Hlas* ("The Voice"), which became a focal point for Slovak emancipation and Slovak-Czech co-operation.

One of the early "Hlasists" was a young Catholic priest, F. Andrew Hlinka. An ardent Slovak nationalist, he formed in 1905, together with Francis Skyčák, the People's party, which for the next forty years was to have a very important place in Slovak political life. For his convictions, Hlinka was severely persecuted. In 1907, he was accused by Bishop Alexander Párvy of an ecclesiastical misdemeanour and suspended from his Ružomberok pastorate. (The charges were eventually dismissed as quite unsubstantiated by the Roman Curia.) In the same year he was charged with treason and sentenced to three-and-a-half years' imprisonment, a great part of which he served in Szeged gaol, where most of the leading Slovak politicians of the day were incarcerated at one time or another, for longer or shorter periods. Indirectly F. Hlinka had been the innocent cause of the Černová massacre, on October 27, 1907. It was the Sharpsville of the Slovak fight for national recognition. Černová was Hlinka's birthplace, and the refusal of the authorities to postpone the dedication of a church there until he himself could perform the ceremony (he being just then both under ecclesiastical suspension and temporal sentence of imprisonment) led to a vocal, but not at all dangerous, protest demonstration. Nevertheless, the Magyar magistrate on the spot ordered the gendarmes to open fire: fifteen of the Černová people were shot dead, and some sixty wounded.

The Černová massacre aroused world-wide indignation. More than anything else it internationalized the Slovak problem. It particularly

affected the Czechs, making them set off the plight of the Slovaks in
Hungary against their own political gains in Austria. In its turn, the
Hungarian government reaped the bitter harvest of its Magyarization
policy when the Great War broke upon it in 1914.

LIBERATION

The Czech and Slovak national movements of the First World War
operated in two quite different environments, and consequently proceeded differently for the greater part of the four years the war lasted;
only toward the end did they join forces openly and unequivocally.
Abroad, the aim practically from the beginning was Czechoslovak independence, to be achieved through vigorous diplomatic and military
support of the Allied powers. At home, an Austrian solution, embody-
ing full national autonomy for the Czechs and Slovaks, was sought for
a long time. This does not mean that the domestic and exile political
leaderships were not in close contact, let alone that they were opposed
to one another. On the contrary, there was excellent co-operation,
mainly through the Prague-based "Maffia." (This term did not have
the derogatory meaning it has in North America, but simply signified
a secret society.) Broadly speaking, the objectives of the domestic resistance represented a minimal solution, those of the exile a maximal.
A compromise between the two would have been possible until the
last year of the war, had the Budapest government ever wanted to
allow it, or the Vienna government been capable of helping work it
out, when at long last it had brought itself to consider it. The Allies did
not want to dismember Austria-Hungary. The Czechs and Slovaks
would not have insisted on it, provided they had been given their due.
It was the action—or inaction—of Budapest and Vienna which made
the ultimate dissolution of the empire inevitable.

It is not possible—or necessary—to describe here in any detail the
wartime struggle of the Czechs and Slovaks for their national goals.
Suffice it to say that, abroad, a leadership triumvirate soon took hold
of the movement, with Professor Masaryk as its head, and Dr. Edward
Beneš, a Czech political economist, and Milan Štefánik, a Slovak astro-
nomer and soldier, as his closest collaborators. A Czechoslovak

National Council was established. Czechoslovak legions, numbering eventually 128,000 men, were put into the field. And, patiently but determinedly, the political job was done of persuading the Allied governments of the justice of the Czech and Slovak national claims (which was comparatively easy), and of the merits of an independent Czechoslovakia as the final solution (which was very difficult).

The Czechoslovak Legion raised in Russia was by far the strongest of the three that were organized (the other two were in France and Italy). On the Russian front, Czech and Slovak soldiers of the Austro-Hungarian Army surrendered in great numbers or, when opportunity offered, went over *en masse* to their Slavic brothers to form themselves into military units fighting on the Allied side. When the front disintegrated in 1917, it was decided to transfer the Czechoslovak Legion to France. The short westward route being blocked by the victorious Germans and Austro-Hungarians, there remained only the 5000-mile eastward journey along the Trans-Siberian railroad to Vladivostok. The long line of Legion trains was moving in that direction when the Russian Civil War started. The Czechoslovaks wanted to stay aloof, but their hand was forced by the Soviets who demanded their disarmament. The first shots were exchanged at a railway siding at Cheljabinsk, in mid-May 1918. To ensure its retreat to Vladivostok, the Legion made itself master of the Trans-Siberian Railroad. There followed a continuous rearguard action as the Czechoslovak echelons proceeded eastward through territory that was at time friendly but just as often inimical. It was a fantastic voyage: Lloyd George called it "one of the greatest epics in history"; President Poincaré of France described it as an "anabasis" (after the original Greek march more than two thousand years earlier described by Xenophon), "an incomparable example of moral strength, endurance and patriotic faith." As the Anabasis, the march of the Legion from the Volga to the Pacific Ocean has gone into Czechoslovak history.

At home, a period of harsh suppression under martial law, during which most of the Czech and Slovak leaders were imprisoned and numbers of lesser people executed as traitors, was followed by one in which attempts were made by the Vienna (but not the Budapest) government to placate the discontented nationalities. Emperor Francis Joseph, who had ruled for a disastrous sixty-eight years, died in November 1916. The new emperor, Charles, destined to be the last of the Habsburg dynasty, called the Reichsrat into session again after a hiatus of three years, and at its opening, on May 30, 1917, the Czech Club demanded "a federal state of free national states with equal rights," and unity for the Czechs and Slovaks. It was to be the last call of this kind. The impasse was indissoluble, with the Czechs insisting on freedom for the Slovaks whom the Magyars would not let go. From then on, the language of even the domestic Czech and Slovak leaders changed. At the Epiphany Convention in Prague, on January 6, 1918, there was already a demand for an independent Czechoslovak state, to be represented as such at the Peace Conference. And when, finally, with the Dual Monarchy *in extremis,* Emperor Charles issued the Manifesto of October 17, 1918, transforming the country into a federation of four states, of the Germans, Czechs, Ukrainians, and Jugoslavs, respectively, the Czechoslovak National Committee in Prague, under the chairmanship of Dr. Charles Kramář, rejected the plan out of hand. Nothing else could have been expected. Not only did the offer come too late—perhaps as much as seventy years too late—but it still did not include the Slovaks, and was thus unacceptable to the Czechs in any case.

Abroad, the Czechoslovak National Council had made slow headway. True, as late as January 5, 1918, Lloyd George spoke for the principal allies when he stated that "the break-up of Austria-Hungary is not part of our war aims." But then the outlook changed. On June 28, 1918, France recognized the Czechoslovak National Council formally as the "supreme organ of the nation, and the first basis of a future Czechoslovak government." Great Britain, and then the United States, followed suit. On October 18, the Council proclaimed itself the provisional government of Czechoslovakia, with Masaryk as premier, Beneš as foreign minister, and Štefánik as minister of war. Ten days later, on October 28, 1918, the Republic was solemnly proclaimed in Prague.

There was never any doubt in the minds of the Slovak leaders that in the wartime national movement they would make common cause with the Czechs. Abroad, Milan Štefánik was one of the leadership triumvirate of the Czechoslovak National Council. At home, there was always co-ordination between the men who guided the two brother nations—a co-ordination limited by adverse circumstances in times of repression, complete when, at least in the Austrian part of the empire, it was possible to act more or less openly. This relaxation of pressure was used to good advantage by the Slovaks, for instance by a group comprising, among others, the veteran leader Dr. Milan Hodža, who worked out of Vienna. In Hungary, of course, any Slovak activities had always to be conducted underground. They were carried on, though, despite the attendant dangers, with two of the principal Slovak leaders, F. Andrew Hlinka and Vavro Šrobár, then working hand-in-hand in Ružomberok. Thus all was ready when the day of liberation arrived, and the first common government of Czechs and Slovaks was established.

Not quite as wholehearted, at any rate not from the start, was the relationship between the Czechoslovak National Council and the most important organization of expatriate Slovaks, the Slovak League in the United States. The latter was certainly less forward in its support of the council than the parallel Czecho-American organizations, the Czech National Alliance and the Union of Czech Catholics. What differences there were, however, were ironed out in the Cleveland Agreement of 1915, and definitively in the Pittsburgh Agreement of May 30, 1918. Both, in broad terms, envisaged a federal state of the Czechs and the Slovaks, but naturally left the working out of an actual constitution of the future common state to the duly elected representatives of its citizens. Much political capital was later made of the two pacts by Slovak opposition forces in the times of the Republic. Sight must not be lost, however, of the fact that the two agreements in question were as between United States citizens of Czech and Slovak origin. They were thus significant mainly because they assured the Czechoslovak National Council of the support of strong, vital, and nationally conscious emigrant groups.

What really mattered—mattered politically in the new state—was that the Slovaks formally sealed their union with the Czechs at a meeting of the Slovak National Committee in Turčiansky Svätý Martin, on October 29 and 30, 1918. It declared unanimously for the

Czechoslovak Republic. Most importantly, it stated the fundamental cause for the union of the two brother nations in its final resolution: "The Slovak nation is linguistically and historically a part of the unitary Czechoslovak nation. In all the cultural struggles fought by the Czech nation, the Slovaks had their share." The word "all" was an excusable exaggeration, but the basic fact was indisputable. The proclamation of the Czechoslovak Republic in Prague, and the Declaration of Turčiansky Svätý Martin, were the necessary historical consequences of a common destiny which had endured despite a thousand years of political separation. Blood being thicker than water, the Czechs and the Slovaks finally got together because they belonged together.

THE GOOD YEARS

OF THE FIRST REPUBLIC

The twenty years of the First Republic were a period of rapid progress for the Czechs and Slovaks, in all fields of endeavour. Economic advances were considerable, especially in Slovakia where a good deal of ground had to be made up. Educational standards increased rapidly. The arts and letters flourished. A complete system of social legislation was enacted which gave to the people a degree of security such as was not achieved in Canada, for instance, until some twenty years later. A great land reform program provided homesteads for some 600,000 landless farm families. The franchise was the widest practicable, and the electoral system of proportionate representation so eminently fair that it had, if anything, an unfavourable effect on political stability, since many small political groupings could be represented in parliament. Minority rights were scrupulously observed. It is no exaggeration to say that, in its institutions, Czechoslovakia was a model republic, a well-nigh perfect democracy.

This is not to say that mistakes were not made, some of them grievous. Most of them sprang from a lack of experience in using political power; often there was a doctrinaire approach to problems which might have been better solved by compromise. This was particularly apparent in the first eight years of the Republic when many of the leaders were still learning to carry political responsibility. Thus, excessive dogmatism accounted for certain anti-clerical tendencies offensive to a deeply religious people, apart from being impolitic in a country almost 75 per cent Catholic, and especially for a centralism which failed to take account of the fact that, however closely related racially and linguistically, the Czechs and Slovaks were, after all, two distinct national groups. The notion of a single Czechoslovak nation (brought up, as was pointed out, in the Declaration of Turčiansky Svätý Martin) may have been ideal in a predominantly Slavic country in which, however, non-Slavs, Germans, and Magyars, accounted for approximately 28 per cent of the population. But it was not a practical notion when the two principal Slavic components had only just joined together after so many centuries of separation.

These initial aberrations were, however, largely cured when, toward the end of 1926, a middle-of-the-road coalition came into power under Anthony Švehla, a particularly able and wise politician. It contained for the first time two cabinet ministers representing the activist German parties, which in turn were supported by the majority of the Sudeten German voters; and two other cabinet ministers representing the People's party of F. Andrew Hlinka, which was, broadly speaking, Slovak autonomist. One of these two was F. Joseph Tiso, who was to become, in the most critical days of the Republic, the party's leader after F. Hlinka's death. Under Švehla, Czechoslovakia rid itself of the tinge of anti-clericalism, concluding, in January 1928, a *modus vivendi* with the Vatican. And the Administrative Law of 1927 brought on a measure of desirable decentralization. Three "countries" were established on lines broadly similar to Canadian provinces, Bohemia, Moravia/Silesia, and Slovakia. Each had its provincial president and its provincial assembly. Subcarpathian Ruthenia, the easternmost and most backward province, had a special status. It had joined Czechoslovakia by the Declaration of Union of May 8, 1919, having been assured the "widest autonomy compatible with the unity of the Republic."

Czechoslovakia seemed on the way toward co-operative, equitable solutions to whatever domestic problems there still were, when two circumstances came to put a brake on this peaceable development: the growth of radicalism in the Slovak People's Party, and the rise of Nazism in Germany.

Slovak autonomism, which in the end turned into Slovak separatism, has to be seen in perspective. It was never anywhere near being a majority movement in Slovakia, the People's party polling in the four general elections held in pre-war Czechoslovakia (1921, 1925, 1929, 1935) 21, 32, 28, and 26 per cent (30 per cent together with the Slovak National party, with which it was temporarily allied in an autonomist bloc) of the Slovak vote, respectively. Furthermore, it was, at any rate until F. Hlinka's death in August 1938, anti-Prague but not anti-Czechoslovak. There were, however, always isolated radical elements among its leadership, and in the thirties an organized radical wing of younger party members formed around the review *Nástup*. The "Nástupists" began with resenting, and strongly criticizing, what they called Czech infiltration into Slovakia, conveniently forgetting that in the first years it had been necessary to put numbers of Czech civil servants and teachers into positions which could not otherwise have been filled: as a result of fifty years of ruthless Magyarization, there were in the beginning simply not enough qualified Slovaks to look after all tasks. What imbalance there was would, however, have eventually righted itself, as the new Slovak secondary schools and the new Slovak university in Bratislava produced enough graduates with the requisite skills. Later, the Nástupists became impressed with the authoritarian ideas emanating from Germany and Italy. It was then that they turned into outright opponents of the Republic.

Having attained power in Germany, Hitler proceeded to spread the National-Socialist creed also among Germans outside the borders of the Reich. In this, he had startling success. Nazism was, in fact, the German ethos of the time, with which not only benighted fanatics but also many otherwise decent and thoughtful Germans became imbued. Among the Sudeten Germans of Czechoslovakia, the transformation from political activism in a state which they had come to accept as their fatherland to rabid nationalism and enmity toward the Republic was particularly fast. In the elections of 1929, the two Sudeten German nationalist parties had polled only about 22 per cent of the Sudeten German vote; in those of 1935, the new unitary nationalist German Home Front (soon afterwards renamed Sudeten German party) was supported by 62 per cent of the German electorate. The rise of Hitler in Germany had made all that difference. The leader of what was now in fact a German *irredenta* in Czechoslovakia was Konrad Henlein, a man who had shown his colour in 1931 by declaring "war to the death on liberalism."

In 1935, at the time of the last general elections, Czechoslovakia was already an island of democracy surrounded by a sea of dictatorships of varying fascist hues. The position was dangerous, the more so as Czechoslovakia not only remained faithful to her democratic principles but also firmly attached to her old international ties. Her foreign policy, which was more high-minded than was healthy in those cynical and corrupt times, was founded on her unswerving support of, and loyalty to, the League of Nations; on the Little Entente, in which she had been linked since the early twenties with Jugoslavia and Rumania; and on her treaty of alliance with France, concluded in January 1924. There was later also a defensive pact with the Soviet Union, of May 16, 1935, which, however, was contingent on a Franco-Soviet master treaty's first becoming operative—in other words, Russia was bound to come to Czechoslovakia's assistance only if and when France fulfilled her previous treaty obligation. The security of Czechoslovakia, threatened by Germany, Hungary, and also, rather foolishly, by Poland because of the trifling Těšín dispute, thus depended substantially on France. Once this pillar crumbled, Czechoslovakia's fate was sealed, for she was then left alone in the midst of her enemies.

MUNICH

AND GERMAN DOMINATION

This is precisely what happened. That it would was not foreseen, and perhaps could not have been foreseen, either by President Beneš who had succeeded the President-Liberator, Thomas Garrigue Masaryk, who had resigned in 1935 (and died in September 1937), or by the Czechoslovak government, by then headed by the veteran Slovak leader, Dr. Milan Hodža. The blow came unexpectedly, brutally, in the course of that tragic concatenation of events which culminated in late September 1938 in the Munich pact—the abject surrender of the great European democracies, Great Britain and France, to the dictators, Hitler and Mussolini.

The Munich pact, as a result of which Czechoslovakia was reduced to a torso indefensible militarily and incapable of life politically, was a tragedy not only for Czechoslovakia, because it made her final extinction within a few months inevitable, but also for the whole world because it was one of the last, and probably the most potent, of a series of fuses which brought on the ultimate explosion of the Second World War. Even greater (because longer lasting) for the Czechs and Slovaks was the psychological impact of Munich. It was a traumatic shock for a people who had courageously stood as the last outpost of democracy in east-central Europe to see themselves coerced not only by inimical tyrannies but by supposedly friendly democracies. For what made surrender without a fight necessary was not so much the wild threats of death and destruction uttered by Hitler as the ultimata which the French and the British ambassadors handed to President Beneš at the unusual hour of 2 a.m., on September 22, 1938. "If the Czechoslovak Government is unable to accept forthwith the Franco-British proposals," it said in the French note (the British was somewhat more guarded but just as unmistakable in its meaning), "and if war results, it is Czechoslovakia who will be responsible for it. . . ." The "Franco-British proposals" were that Czechoslovakia should give in to Hitler's demands. To assign beforehand the responsibility for a possible world war to the victim of aggression, was surely the most insidious—and the most effective—way of ensuring the latter's compliance.

Less than a year later, France and Great Britain, who had thrown Czechoslovak democracy to the wolves, went to war in defence of a totalitarian Poland. Political developments ordained it that way, but to the average Czech and Slovak this must have appeared as sheer cynicism, as proof that in international politics it does not pay to be good. The bitter disappointment over Munich has burned deeply into the souls of the Czechs and Slovaks. This explains much of what they did, or may have failed to do, in subsequent years. Though diminished by the passage of time, the memory of Munich is, in the national life, still a factor to be reckoned with.

Poland and Hungary were the subsidiary beneficiaries of the Munich dictate. The former seized somewhat more than the area around Těšín it had claimed; the latter received from Germany and Italy, through the so-called Vienna Award of November 2, 1938, important parts of Slovakia and Subcarpathian Ruthenia.

The Slovak autonomists, too, used the opportunity provided by the political defeat of Czechoslovakia to further their aims. A meeting in Žilina of the executive committee of the Slovak People's party was used to stage a political coup. A manifesto was issued on October 6, 1938 proclaiming the autonomy of Slovakia within the Republic. At the same time the party also ranged itself on the side of "those fighting against the Marxist-Jewish ideology of disorganization and violence." Ferdinand Ďurčanský, minister of justice in the first autonomous government of Slovakia, made quite sure that the meaning of that policy was clearly understood when, a few days later, in Berlin, he assured Reichsmarshal Hermann Goering that in Slovakia "the Jewish question will be settled in the same way as in Germany." Other totalitarian habits and trappings were gradually adopted. Opposition —of still the great majority of the Slovaks if they only had been allowed to voice it—was cowed by the armed Hlinka Guards, untouchable because behind them stood the equally armed Ordners of the remaining German minority in Slovakia, and behind the latter the might of Nazi Germany. Sham elections were held, in which only a single list of candidates, drawn up by the People's party, was submitted to the voters. Predictably, it was announced that it had been endorsed by 99 per cent of the electorate.

The stage was thus set for the last act of the drama. In connivance with, if not at the straight order of, Berlin, an independent Slovak State was proclaimed on March 14, 1939, although not even the majority of the People's party members really wanted it. "Without the pressure exercised by Hitler," said F. Joseph Tiso, the first and only president of the Slovak State, at his trial after the war, "the Slovak Diet would never have voted in favour of the independence of Slovakia." The following night, German troops marched into the Czech areas. The Protectorate of Bohemia-Moravia was established headed by a German protector, under whom Dr. Emil Hácha, a distinguished Czech jurist, served as president of a very limited, internal

John Amos Komenský (Comenius)   John Hus

Hvězda Castle on the White Mountain near Prague,
site of the Czechs' last stand, 1620

Milan Štefánik

Thomas Garrigue Masaryk

The Old City Hall in Prague

Miroslav Tyrš

Edward Beneš

Karlštejn Castle in Bohemia

Czech self-government. The Hungarians occupied what was left of Subcarpathian Ruthenia. The First Republic of Czechoslovakia was no more.

Although in complete subjection, and treated, if anything, a little worse than the somewhat more privileged German-occupied countries such as Norway or Belgium, the Czechs in the end fared better in their wretched protectorate than the Slovaks in their ostensibly independent state. At least, they were not required to fight for Germany and there was no fratricidal conflict: except for the actions of a few quislings, all oppression came at the hands of the Germans. In Slovakia, on the other hand, the majority of the nation was forced by a radical minority onto a highly unpopular pro-German course. "We chose a German orientation," said F. Tiso at the Convention of the People's party in Trenčín, on October 1, 1939, "and we shall continue along this path, because we believe in this orientation. . . . I assured Hitler that he would never be disappointed in the Slovak State."

The result was that two Slovak divisions, numbering at one time with supporting and corps troops upward of 50,000, fought in the German ranks on the Russian front; and one division, used admittedly only for logistic services, on the Italian. The Slovak state joined the tri-partite pact of the great totalitarian powers, Germany, Italy, and Japan. It declared war on Great Britain and the United States. And during the uprising in 1944, Slovaks faced Slovaks, even though German troops bore the brunt of the fighting against the Slovak patriots. It is not for seeking Slovak independence that the leaders of the People's party must be blamed so much as for splitting the nation. They did to Slovakia what the Vichy French did to France, with the same disastrous results.

As in the First World War, the Czechoslovak liberation movement was directed from abroad by a Czechoslovak National Committee formed in Paris in 1939 and transformed one year later, in London, into a full-fledged Czechoslovak government-in-exile under the leadership of President Edward Beneš. At home, underground resistance groups organized themselves both in the protectorate and in Slovakia. Under generally more adverse conditions, the Czech Resistance was the less spectacular, although it provided the Allies with much useful intelligence and there was a good deal of scattered sabotage. The assassination of the acting protector, the infamous SS chief Reinhard Heydrich, in 1942, followed by the terrible bloodbath the Germans staged in reprisal, showed to the world that the Czechs had by no means knuckled down.

In Slovakia, two parallel resistance movements had sprung up, one democratic headed by John Ursíny, and one leftist, composed of Social Democrats and Communists, but with the latter gradually gaining the upper hand, in which Gustav Husák became the leading personality. They eventually joined forces at Christmas 1943, declaring themselves unequivocally for the reconstitution of the Czechoslovak Republic, and resolving to "conduct affairs in agreement with the Czechoslovak Government (in exile) and the liberation movement." The thus united Slovak National Council established a military command under Lieutenant-Colonel John Golian, and in the late summer of 1944, with the Soviet armies within about a hundred miles, went over to open action. During two months, from the end of August to the end of October 1944, the Slovak National Council was in control of virtually the whole of central and eastern Slovakia. There were Communists active in the Slovak national uprising, both in the political leadership and in the fighting ranks, but they were definitely in the minority: four in the original Council of thirteen, and thirteen in the ultimate one of fifty members. The Council's army, the First Czechoslovak, commanded by Golian, now a general, and later by General Rudolf Viest, dispatched by the Czechoslovak government-in-exile in London, battled heroically against a crushingly superior force of German regular troops, supported by Hlinka Guards and Ordners. The expected Soviet support was not forthcoming: only an under-strength Czechoslovak Parachute Brigade serving with the Soviet forces was belatedly brought in, as well as some partisans. Any large-scale help from the West was prevented by Moscow. In that respect the Slovak national uprising did not fare any better than the somewhat earlier Warsaw uprising, and undoubtedly for the same reason: it was not a communist revolt, and the Kremlin was thus not interested in it succeeding. Yet even after defeat, and despite bloody German reprisals, smaller Slovak units continued to fight a guerilla war right to the final overthrow, in April 1945, of the ill-fated and ill-conceived Slovak state and of its German overlords.

THE SHORT-LIVED
SECOND REPUBLIC

By May 9, 1945, with Germany defeated, the Second Czechoslovak Republic was born. Alas, it was not the starry-eyed, idealistic product of Masarykian liberalism, but rather of laboured political compromise arrived at under heavy Soviet pressure. It was compromise necessitated by the circumstance that Czechoslovakia was in a divided Europe assigned to the Soviet zone of control; the compromise was embodied in the Košice Program of April 5, 1945, which represented the maximum that could be attained by democratic leaders faced by communists who had Soviet bayonets to back them. Still, a somewhat limited democracy could have developed, not perfect and not comparable to that of the First Republic, but one in which Czech and Slovak people could have lived in freedom, secure under the law. If this did not come to pass, it was because Moscow did not want it to happen and had in the Czechoslovak communists the instrument with which to enforce its will.

We are now in the realm of recent history, and so can be brief. From May 1945 to February 1948, the democratic parties waged a rearguard action against relentless, insidious, sometimes violent, communist encroachment. Understandably perhaps, considering that Czechoslovakia was liberated in the main by Soviet armies and that the memories of Munich and the German occupation were still fresh, the Communist party had strong popular support, but they were far from being in the majority. In May 1946, in the only free general elections held in the Second Republic they got anywhere from 40 per cent of the vote in Bohemia to 30 per cent in Slovakia, 38 per cent over all. How great their strength was in February 1948, when they seized power in a political coup, we shall never know, for they did not put it to the test of the polling booth. At any rate, by February 25, they were in effective control of the country. The constitution of May 9, 1948, on the Soviet pattern, established the Third Republic, called the Czecho-Slovak Socialist. On June 7, President Beneš resigned. Three months later he died, eleven years after his great mentor.

It was the end of an era, but only of one of a number through which the Czechs and Slovaks have gone, in happiness and in sorrow. They live on, together in their common homeland, with their national fibre unimpaired and their sense of unity unshaken despite all the vicissitudes it has been their fate to encounter in the eleven centuries of their recorded history.

Such then, in very broad outline, is the background of the two fraternal peoples, the story of whose sons and daughters in Canada we are about to tell in this book.

Bibliography

AULNEAU, J., *Histoire de l'Europe centrale*, Paris, 1926.
BRUCE-LOCKHARDT, R. H., *Guns or Butter*, London, 1942.
ČAPEK, THOMAS, *The Slovaks of Hungary*, New York, 1906.
DE BRAY, R. G. A., *Guide to Slavonic Languages*, London, New York, 1951.
DENIS, ERNEST, *Les Slovaques*, Paris, 1917.
DVORNÍK, FRANTIŠEK, *Les Slaves, Byzance et Rome au IXe siècle*, Paris, 1926.
—— *The Making of Central and Eastern Europe*, London, 1949.
HEATON, H., *An Economic History of Europe* (rev. ed.), New York, 1948.
HODŽA, MILAN, *Federation in Central Europe*, London, 1942.
JÁSZI, O., *The Dissolution of the Hapsburg Monarchy*, Chicago, 1929.
KERNER, J. (ed.), *Czechoslovakia*, Berkeley, Calif., 1945.
KIRSCHBAUM, J., *Slovakia's Struggle for Independence*, Toronto, 1959.
KROFTA, KAMIL, *Histoire de la Tchécoslovaquie*, Brussels, 1930.
—— *A Short History of Czechoslovakia*, New York, 1934.
LETTRICH, JOZEF, *History of Modern Slovakia*, New York, 1955.
MASARYK, T. G., *The Making of A State*, London, 1927.
MAY, J. ARTHUR, *The Hapsburg Monarchy, 1867–1914*, Cambridge, Mass., 1951.
MÚDRY-ŠEBÍK, M., *Short History of the Slovaks*, Pittsburg, Pa., 1940.
ODDO, L. GILBERT, *Slovakia and Its People*, New York, 1960.
OPOČENSKÝ, J., *The Collapse of the Austro-Hungarian Monarchy and the Rise of the Czechoslovak State*, Prague, 1928.
SETON-WATSON, R. W., *Slovakia Then and Now—The New Slovakia*, Prague, 1924.
—— *Slovakia Then and Now*, London, 1931.
—— *A History of the Czechs and Slovaks*, London, 1943.
STEED, HENRY WICKHAM, *The Habsburg Monarchy*, London, 1913.
STREET, C. J. C., *Hungary and Democracy*, London, 1923.
—— *Slovakia Past and Present*, London, 1928.
THOMSON, S. HARRISON, *Czechoslovakia in European History*, Princeton, 1951.
YURCHAK, PETER P., *The Slovaks*, Whiting, Ind., 1946.

CHAPTER TWO

Czech and Slovak settlement in Canada

FIRST CONTACTS
(to 1885)

Before the introduction of steam navigation, North America was very remote from the homeland of the Czechs and Slovaks in east-central Europe. One would be tempted to say that geographically, politically, culturally, they were worlds apart, were there not occasional bits of evidence to show that, even then, ours was one world in which all peoples, however tenuously, were somehow in contact.

These contacts were not, of course, always of much consequence, but there was one which is germane to our subject. Prince Rupert, son of the last elected king of Bohemia, Frederick V of the Palatinate, and of Elizabeth Stuart, daughter of King James I of England, was born in Prague in 1619. He became an exile with his parents only one year later after the Battle of the White Mountain and he never set foot again in the Czech lands. He is said, however, to have retained a few words of Czech, learned probably from his nanny, and he always considered Bohemia his patrimony unjustly taken from him. Although he naturally had no impact on Czech history, he made a considerable one on North American. A charter member of the Hudson's Bay Company, he gave his name to all the Company's lands draining into

Hudson Bay—Rupert's Land—and later to Prince Rupert in British Columbia.

Also fleeting, but more substantial, was an even earlier contact, by Thomas Štitnický, called Parmenius or Budaeus. As there was no Slovakia then, he was called a Hungarian, but his Slovak origin is beyond question. Probably through his academic work, Parmenius came in touch with the famous geographer Richard Hakluyt, Master of Christ Church, Oxford, and later author of the monumental work, *The Principal Navigations, Voyages and Discoveries of the English Nation*. It was no doubt upon Hakluyt's recommendation that Sir Humphrey Gilbert took Parmenius along on his 1583 voyage to North America. His task was "to record in the Latin tongue the gests and things worthy of remembrance happening in this discovery, to the honour of our nation, the same being adorned with the eloquent style of this orator, a rare poet of our time."

Fate did not allow Parmenius to write more than a kind of preface to the intended work, a rhetorical dedication composed before the expedition sailed and entitled, "De navigatione illustris et magnanimi equitis aurati Humfredi Gilberti." For the enterprise ended in disaster. After setting sail in early June 1583, Sir Humphrey anchored in what is now the harbour of St. John's Newfoundland on August 3, and two days later took possession of the land for the Queen. He sailed again a fortnight later. On the night of September 9 the flagship the *Squirrel* foundered in a storm and with it went down both Sir Humphrey Gilbert and Parmenius.

We have, however, a description by Parmenius of the impression Newfoundland made on him. It must be one of the earliest descriptions of the New-found-land, and it is contained in a lengthy letter addressed to Hakluyt, under the date of August 6, 1583: "The manner of this country and people remain now to be spoken of. But what shall I say, my good Hakluyt, when I see nothing but a very wilderness? Of fish here is incredible abundance, whereby great gains grow to them that travel to these parts: the hook is no sooner thrown out but it is drawn up with some good fish. The whole land is full of hills and woods." Hardly a place to inspire an "eloquent" "orator" to great outbursts of enthusiasm!

The first real link between the Czechs and Slovaks and the lands which later became Canada was fashioned by missionaries of the Moravian Church, and it proved to be a lasting one. The story of the Moravians in North America is important enough in Canadian history to be treated here in some detail.

The Moravian Church, formally established by the Covenant of all its Brethren of August 13, 1727, is the direct offspring, indeed a continuation under a different name, of the Unity of the Brethren (Unitas Fratrum, or Czech Brethren) founded by Brother Gregory in Kunvald in 1457. This Church can thus claim to be part of the oldest Reformed Church in Christendom. After the Battle of the White Mountain, the Brethren were suppressed. The Counter-Reformation failed, however, to extirpate altogether the "hidden seed," the underground practice of the religion. A particularly resistant group of Brethren held on tenaciously to their faith, despite all persecution, in Northern Moravia. In 1722, more than one hundred years after the White Mountain, the group still existed. In that year, it sought and was given refuge in Protestant Saxony, under the protection of Count Nicholas Louis Zinzendorf.

The count, twenty-two years old at the time and a Pietist, later became a famous and influential German religious and social reformer. To the Moravians, whom the "Moravian Moses," the carpenter Christian David of Ženklava near Štramberk, had led out of their homeland, Zinzendorf assigned a corner of his estate of Berthelsdorf. There the fugitives founded the community of Herrnhut, "the Lord's protection." It was also here that the Covenant of 1727 was signed, and here that eight years later the first bishop of the Church, David Nitschmann of Kunvald, was consecrated by Bishop Daniel Ernest Jablonský, the grandson of the greatest of the Czech Brethren, John Amos Komenský. The Moravian Church was, incidentally, recognized by an Act of the British Parliament of 1749 as "an ancient Protestant episcopal Church." This proved of value when the Brethren extended their missionary work throughout the British domains in North America.

That the Moravian Church should have seized upon missionary work in faraway lands almost immediately after its formal establishment in Herrnhut is in itself a curiosity—the Brethren, in the main simple, small-town artisans, could hardly have known of the wide world beyond the horizon. Yet, even though they pitted themselves against the greatest possible difficulties, material as well as human, the Moravians became the most successful of Protestant missionaries.

It all started with a mission to the Greenland Eskimos. The impulse for it was given to Count Zinzendorf during a visit he paid to the Court of Denmark. There, he met a Danish missionary, Hans Egede, just returned from a frustrating ten years in inhospitable Greenland (1721 to 1731), during which he had made little headway with the instruction, let alone the conversion, of the natives. It must have occurred to Egede that perhaps he had failed because he had attempted a purely spiritual, a preacher's, approach to a people totally absorbed in the struggle for survival, a people who furthermore felt that in that struggle they were vastly superior to the fragile stranger who proposed to lead them. Thus, lack of respect for the bearer transferred itself to the message, and failure necessarily ensued.

At any rate, if this realization did not come to Egede, it certainly came to Zinzendorf, who despite his absorbing preoccupation with religion remained the typical forceful and imperious nobleman of his days. It struck him that a more muscular form of Christianity might succeed where the entirely evangelical approach had failed. This kind of thinking probably led Zinzendorf to offer to send out a lay mission, composed of pious but not learned practical men of peasant stock, to aid the theologian Egede. And quite naturally, then, the choice fell upon the Herrnhut Moravians. This the more so as the latters' nonconformism was just at that time causing certain difficulties.

The honour of leading the first missionary expedition to foreign lands fell naturally upon the head of the community, the "Moravian Moses," Christian David. He was accompanied by the cousins Matthew and Christian Stach, both of Suchdol in Moravia. Matthew, the one who eventually persevered in Greenland and became the moving spirit of the later Labrador enterprise, had come out of Moravia when he was ten, in the original trek led by Christian David. There is no doubt that by nationality he was Czech: he habitually spoke Czech, although having received his schooling in Saxony, he could write only in German. In this, he was typical of the early Moravian Brethren. Later generations were completely Germanized.

The three left Herrnhut in early 1733, and went on foot across Germany to Copenhagen. They were briefly delayed there—King Christian VI of Denmark was not at all impressed at first by the three simple men attempting a proselytizing mission which had stumped a learned cleric—but by April 1733 they were allowed to sail in the *Caritas*. They reached Godthaab, Greenland, at the end of May.

What happened to the Moravian missionaries in Greenland is not germane to this story. Suffice it to say that they encountered, apart from the awesome physical obstacles to be expected in the far north, also great spiritual difficulties. Not the least of their burdens was Egede himself, a visionary and doctrinaire who wanted to see all activities in the colony, social as well as economic, subordinated to the missionary work. He, Christian David, and Christian Stach gave up, exhausted and dispirited by successive setbacks, but Matthew Stach held on, directing the work of the Greenland mission for thirty-eight years.

Matthew Stach found new helpers through his sister Anne: the latter's husband, Frederick Boehnisch of Kunvald, and a Moravian Brother from Germany, John Beck. Stach was ordained a presbyter of the Church. The first few Eskimo converts were baptised. And a Moravian community, New Herrnhut, was founded, followed later by two more.

What concerns us here is the extension of the Moravians' work to the Eskimos across the Davis Strait in Labrador. A first abortive attempt had been made in 1752 by Moravian Brethren from England led by John Christian Ehrhardt, but the first of the Labrador missions founded from Greenland was not established until 1771, the year of Matthew Stach's retirement. Still, this mission at Nain was his spiritual child; he had given the first impulse. In Greenland, before their departure for Labrador, he had trained the men who ultimately succeeded, the Danes, Haven and Drachart. And he had imbued these men with the principles on which the Moravian communities in Greenland were run, so much so that the early Labrador missions were replicas of Stach's. After Nain, the Moravian mission of Okkak was founded in 1776, and that of Hopedale in 1782. More were established later, and some have survived to our days, still prospering and doing devoted work.

They have, of course, long ceased to be Czech or Slovak establishments. These days, the life-centre of the Moravian Church is in North America; the old spiritual spring in Czechoslovakia, while by no means dried out, has flowed weakly since the death of Kamil Nagy, Senior of the Synod of the Evangelical Church of the Czech Brethren, in Prague in September 1939. The missionaries, who still work in many lands, are of all nationalities now. Only a small minority among them are Czechs and Slovaks. Yet some of the old Czech core has remained throughout the 240 years since the signing of the Herrnhut Covenant. Thus, when the Reverend Benjamin La Trobe visited the Moravian settlement at Hebron Bay, Labrador, in September 1888, two of the four missionaries, good "gentlemen in sealskin coats," whom he found there had names suggesting they must have been of Czech origin.

Shortly after Christian David and the two Stachs left for Greenland, a more important expedition of Moravian missionaries was mounted, whose task was to work among the Indians in the British colonies on the Atlantic seaboard of North America. They sailed in two groups. The first, in 1734, was led by August Gottlieb Spangenberg, formerly professor of theology at Jena and Halle, later author of the compendium of the Church's doctrine (*Idea fidei Fratrum*), and finally Count Zinzendorf's successor as the acknowledged leader of the Moravian Brethren. In his party of ten, there were eight who originally came from Moravia. A bigger group of twenty-five followed in November 1735. At its head was the new bishop of the Moravian Church, David Nitschmann of Kunvald. Again, the majority of the members were from Moravia and Bohemia. Among them was a lad of fourteen, who was destined to put the imprint of his personality on all the missionary work of the Church in North America, David Zeissberger. Born in Suchdol, Moravia, he was one year old when his parents brought him to Herrnhut in Christian David's trek.

The Moravians first gained a foothold in Georgia, then gradually extended their activities northward, into the Carolinas, Pennsylvania, and Ohio. Again, their story, as far as it unfolded in what later became the United States of America, does not belong in this volume. We must thus skip the next forty years, and resume our account in 1775, at the outbreak of the American War of Independence.

At that time, David Zeissberger, who because of his work has been justly called the "apostle of the Delaware Indians," headed the Church's western missions from a headquarters in Tuscarawas County, Ohio. The Moravians, themselves dedicated pacifists, had (as Francis Parkman pointed out) "succeeded to a surprising degree in weaning their Indian converts from their ferocious instincts and war-like habits." Quite naturally, then, they were determined to remain neutral in the fighting between the British and the American colonists, proclaiming "We will not go to war and will not buy anything from warriors that was taken in war." Just as naturally, they were ground between the millstones as a result. To the Americans generally every Indian was a bad Indian, even such peaceable and settled groups as the Christian Delawares. Indians could expect little mercy if they fell into American hands.

With the war coming closer to Tuscarawas County, Zeissberger had no option but to take sides after all, by putting his flock under British protection. That his apprehensions were not at all exaggerated was tragically proven in March 1782, when ninety of his Indians, men, women and children, innocent of the slightest offence, were seized by General Williamson's United States troops and slaughtered in cold blood.

Once under British protection, Zeissberger's Moravian Brethren and mission Indians were moved to and fro as the fortunes of war varied, along the shifting demarcation line between the British and United States territories: first to Sandusky, off Lake Erie, then to a site near the present town of Mount Clemens, Michigan, and back into Ohio, where the Moravians founded the community of New Salem. The latent danger, however, remained. In 1791, Zeissberger finally applied for definite resettlement of his people at a place some distance inside the British part of North America, to the north of the Great Lakes.

In the spring of that year, then, Zeissberger's group was transported in boats to what is now Amherstburg, Ontario. From there they later marched inland, to a site on the north bank of the River Thames, in Kent County, twenty miles above Chatham, and sixty miles below where the city of London was to be founded thirty-four years later. The party, 151 strong, arrived at that spot on May 3, 1792, and immediately set to work building a church, a school, and the log houses of a village which they named "Fairfield," but which was soon locally known as "Moraviantown." Of it, the local Church diary says under the date of July 28, 1798: "Fairfield is a garden of the Lord in which he has planted many trees which were originally wild. Some have brought forth fruit to His glory; others have as yet produced nothing and are apparently cumberers of the ground." The allegory shows that even amid the saintliness of a Moravian mission community there were the good and the bad.

Fairfield got its charter by Order in Council of July 10, 1793, which allotted approximately fifty thousand acres of the surrounding land as a reserve for the Moravian Indians. Governor John Graves Simcoe came for a visit the following year, stopping overnight on a journey to Detroit. He was duly impressed, and "commended [the settlers] for their thrift and industry." Industrious they certainly were. It is recorded that, among other things, they first introduced bee-keeping into Upper Canada. But alas, the idyll of Fairfield did not last for long. It was destroyed by yet another war, this time that of 1812.

The story of how it came about that Fairfield became the site of a battle demonstrates once again that the destinies of little people are so often decided arbitrarily by the distant and impersonal decisions of the high and mighty. In this case, the fate of the settlement was sealed at a council of war held at Malden after the disastrous Battle of Lake Erie (September 10, 1813), which deprived the British forces on the western border of their principal means of supply and of the protection of the big guns of the fleet. Consequently, the local commander, General Henry Procter, wanted to fall back quickly upon the main body of the army, at Burlington Heights. The chief of his Indian allies, Tecumseh, on the other hand, demanded that a stand be made where they were, around the forts of Detroit and Amherstburg. Had either of these counsels prevailed, Fairfield might have been spared. Instead, a compromise plan was agreed upon. The combined British and Indian force would retreat slowly along the line of the River Thames, precisely as far as Fairfield. Battle would be offered there, if necessary. Militarily, the decision of the war council was a bad one; for the Moravians it spelled disaster.

The Battle of the Thames, or of Moraviantown as it is usually called, was fought a little to the west of Fairfield, on October 5, 1813. Procter was defeated; the Americans pursued him for some fifteen miles, then returned, to burn Fairfield to the ground.

David Zeissberger had died in 1808 and so did not witness this misfortune. But his people, undaunted, returned to the blackened ruins of their village. They rebuilt it, this time on the opposite, south side of the Thames, and called it New Fairfield. The Moravians continued their good work in western Ontario until 1903 when their missionary activities were taken over by the Methodist Church.

We have lingered over this chapter in earlier Canadian history, because, in the context of this book, it seems to have particular significance. What the Moravians did for North America is in a way typical of what the Czechs and Slovaks did for the world. For if they have had any influence on the development of the western world—and, in fact, that influence has been considerable—then it has been in the spiritual field. John Hus, the first Reformed Church, the great teachers and humanists from Comenius to Masaryk—it was they rather than whatever warriors or political leaders the two brother nations have produced, who have made an imprint on history. It is thus within the spirit of the Czech and Slovak past that the first real contact with Canada was made by men of God, and especially by such as the Moravians who personified what was best in the Czech and Slovak national make-up: devotion to ideals, simplicity, compassion, and infinite capacity for suffering. No better first offerings could have been brought to a new country.

THE FORERUNNERS
(1885 to 1918)

Emigration—or leaving the homeland for the purpose of *settling* elsewhere, as distinct from merely looking for work in a foreign country—from the lands of the Czechs and Slovaks really started only after 1860, and in the beginning did not reach out farther than the black-soil land of the Ukraine in one direction, and the coal mines of France in the other. The reasons for moving were the customary ones: first and foremost, economic want, and then political discontent. This second reason was predominant among the Czechs who, materially, were relatively well off in the Austrian part of the Habsburg Empire; the first was the one which drove the Slovaks out of Hungary. As a result, Slovak emigration was much more important than Czech in the half century preceding the outbreak of the First World War.

The Slovaks of Upper Hungary were, in the nineteenth century, chiefly a rural people, and landless at that, since more than 60 per cent of the land was held by big owners, Hungarian or foreign. They soon began to eye the open spaces of North America as a promised land. The words—not very flattering, but true enough in those times—of Emma Lazarus' sonnet inscribed on New York's Statue of Liberty may have been addressed to a good many of those early Slovak immigrants to the United States:

> Give me your tired, your poor,
> Your huddled masses yearning to breathe free,
> The wretched refuse of your teeming shore. . . .

The first of the Slovaks arrived in North America in 1873: it is recorded that "1,300 immigrants came from Hungary" to the United States that year. No doubt the majority of them were Slovaks. Their numbers increased from then on, so much so that by 1880 the Hungarian government had grown alarmed. The means by which modern despotic governments keep their reluctant citizenry from bolting were not yet conceived; and the more primitive methods the Budapest government employed, such as stationing gendarmes at the border of the Austrian half of the empire to question travellers, had little effect when common people taking to the road did not carry travel documents. Thus, between 1881 and 1884, only a decade after serious overseas emigration had started, some Slovak areas lost as much as 5 per cent of their population.

The Czechs, if they emigrated at all, did so individually and selectively. They were generally skilled workers and artisans looking in the new cities of North America for a wider scope for their enterprise than

they could expect to have at home. For one reason or the other, Chicago was their principal goal (it is even now thought to be the third
most populous Czech city in the world) and the Chicago census of
1870 listed 6,277 "Bohemians." At that time, the number of Czechs and
Slovaks in Canada could probably have been counted on the fingers
of one's two hands.

In the following decades, immigration from Austria-Hungary to the
United States increased by leaps and bounds. It had accounted for
one-third of one per cent of the approximately 2.3 million who came in
the 1860s. It made up almost one-quarter of the approximately 8.8
million who streamed into the United States in the first ten years of
the twentieth century. Czechs and Slovaks formed a considerable proportion of the Austro-Hungarian total. To get an idea of what this
meant in demographic terms, one must remember that at present
almost one-third of all Slovaks live abroad, very many in the United
States.

Although at first sight it would not seem part of our subject, immigration to the United States in fact does have a bearing on the Czechs
and Slovaks in Canada, for many of the original settlers came here via
the United States. And the later introduction of a quota system to
govern immigration into the United States made Canada a prime goal
of Czech and Slovak emigrants.

That the first significant influx of Slovaks, and of a few Czechs,
into Canada came not directly from Europe but rather by way of the
United States also explains why it was directed to the Canadian west
and not, as one would have expected, to the more developed east.
The Slovaks had been relatively late in joining the general westward
trek across North America, and before long there was no more
unoccupied land for families whose only working capital was willing
hands and a good dash of optimism. It was at this time that the
Dominion government opened its Crown lands in the prairies and the
Canadian Pacific Railway (CPR) offered to settlers the huge tracts it
had received as land grants. That virtually empty region, through
which the transcontinental railroad wound its forlorn and seemingly
purposeless way, was advertised as "the last, best west." It was indeed
the last, on a continent where the pioneering days were coming to a

close. Perhaps it was the best. At any rate, prospective settlers began to come in droves, many of them from the United States.

The trend started in the early eighties of the nineteenth century. The CPR began its colonization campaign in 1881. A year later, settlement through colonization companies was approved. Broadly speaking, such companies would buy land from the government at a very low price (two dollars an acre, or so), would hopefully make some improvements on it, and then find settlers to whom to resell it. If a company fulfilled its obligations—in the main, getting two settlers for each section of land—the government refunded to it part of the purchase price, anywhere around $120 for each *bona fide* settler. It was through such colonization companies that most of the early Slovak immigrants acquired their land in the Canadian west.

The scheme caught on quickly. By 1883, within a year of its inception, there were twenty-six colonization companies operating in the prairie territories and, between them, they had bought up just under three million acres of land. There were drawbacks, of course. Some of the companies were fly-by-nights which engaged in wild speculation and often folded after having done a great deal of harm. On the other hand, there were some which did all that was expected of them and more, including the building of roads and bridges as part of land improvement. All helped to publicize the west, even if they were not choosy about how they did it. In his *Between the Red and the Rockies*, Grant MacEwan cites an advertisement in a St. Paul, Minnesota, newspaper, which was typical of the style of those irrepressible land hucksters: "Buy farmlands in Saskatchewan. You can leave home after Easter, sow your grain and take in the harvest and come home with your pockets full of money in time for Thanksgiving dinner." Even the Prime Minister, Sir John A. Macdonald, was heard referring to the western bonanza, albeit perhaps with a bit of scepticism: "I am told you can come in on the train in the morning and start ploughing in the afternoon."

Although things were not as rosy as all that, yet, as we now know, the land in the Territories was as good as advertised. Despite the rigours of the climate, it became the world's greatest wheat acreage, for there was already in use in eastern Canada a hardy spring wheat

The Most Illustrious and High Borne Prince Rupert,
Prince Electour Palatine of ye Righne Second Sonne to
Fredericke King of Bohemia Generall of ye Horse of his
Ma:ties Army. Knight of ye Most Noble Order of the Garter: &c

Ant: F. Dyck Pinxit.   Are to be sould by Robt Peake at his Shopp neere Holborne Cunduit.

The church at New Fairfield

St. Peter's Slovak Roman Catholic Parish, founded 1907, Fort William, Ontario

Cranbrook, British Columbia, *circa* 1906

Cemetery at Fernie, British Columbia, 1902, where the victims of the mine disaster lie

which matured early enough even for the short growing season of the prairies. It was "Red Fife," which Duncan Fife had brought to Upper Canada from Scotland early in the century. Thus the pre-Confederation vision of a transcontinental railway, an exceptionally liberal settlement policy, and the availability of the right kind of cash crop, combined to make of the Canadian west, from about 1880 onwards, a veritable Mecca for immigrants.

It is difficult to say who were the first Czech or Slovak settlers in the Canadian west. Probably they were four Czech farm families, the Pangrács, the Juneks, the Doležals, and the Skokans, who came in 1884 to what was then the District of Assiniboia, part of today's Saskatchewan. The little hamlet they founded they called Kolin, after the town in the midst of the rich farmland in central Bohemia from which they seem to have originally come. By all indications, theirs was an adventurous, individualistic enterprise, and not the result of any larger, planned action.

Organized settlement begins with the appearance on the scene of a strange personality who called himself Count Paul Esterhazy. He may or may not have been a scion of that illustrious and powerful Magyar aristocratic family—in 1885, he was accused in some New York newspapers of being an imposter by the name of John Papp— but he was certainly a man who possessed vision, enterprise, and withal, compassion. The idea of trying to organize farm settlements in Canada may have been suggested to him by John Dyke, who opened a colonization and travel bureau in Vienna, the first Canadian agency of that kind in east-central Europe. (At one time, the Dyke organization reputedly employed as many as six hundred agents who recruited immigrants all over Hungary for a bounty of five dollars a head.) Dyke also may have brought Esterhazy into contact with the CPR. At any rate, Esterhazy founded in New York the "First Hungarian-American Colonization Company," which was approved by the CPR which paid its owner a retainer of $70 a month. It was at the invitation of the CPR also that Esterhazy visited Canada, to view the farmlands available for settlement in the province of Manitoba and in the Assiniboia District of the North-West Territories.

The first comprehensive settlement plan which Esterhazy submitted to the Canadian authorities on May 9, 1885, was characteristic of the kind of man he was. What he had hatched out in his imaginative mind was a replica of the Military Frontier which the Habsburgs had established for defence against the Turks, with soldier-farmers acting as an advance border guard. It was not quite clear what foreign dangers a Canadian military frontier was supposed to ward off, although it seems that Esterhazy was thinking of the threat of Russia and of the protection of the empire against encroachment from that quarter. And so he envisaged a long, firm line of settlements of first-class farmers who would at the same time be well-trained soldiers, and he spoke vaguely of some 200,000 and more former Hungarian citizens now resident in the United States who might be prevailed upon to transfer to Canada to perform that noble task.

What Esterhazy in fact achieved was more modest and less romantic, but still quite significant. A temporary depression in the coal-mining industry of eastern Pennsylvania, coupled with some labour unrest, had put a great number of immigrant miners out of work, and in the absence of social security of any kind had made them utterly destitute. Esterhazy gathered thirty-eight miners' families at Hazleton, Pennsylvania, and sent them off on July 30, 1885, via Toronto and Winnipeg, to the Minnedosa region of western Manitoba. The great majority of them were Slovaks, as their names testify: Zinčák and Rosol, Kolesár and Dolejčík, Šimon and Vazil, Kašperik and Čižmár. The group arrived at their destination in August 1885, ahead of two more which came before the winter fell. Their leader was George Doery, from Zemplín county in present-day eastern Slovakia, who up to then had been Esterhazy's right-hand man in the colonization company.

The CPR tided the newcomers over the winter by giving the men of the party jobs on the railroad, and in the spring of 1886 they settled properly on their tract of virgin land. The new community was given the name of Huns' Valley. This may not have been very complimentary, although no offence was intended: the local people had only a very vague idea of where Hungary was and "Hun" was as good an abbreviation as any for Hungarian; and there seemed to be some historic connection, however distant, between Magyars and Huns.

The settlers do not seem to have minded. After all, even the authorities sometimes called them Huns. There is, for instance, in the Sessional Papers of 1887 a report by W. C. B. Graham, government land agent in Winnipeg, with the following reference: "Various European settlers formed colonies throughout the district. These, composed of Germans, Russians, Icelanders, Scandinavians and Huns, seem all well pleased with their location, thrifty and hardworking, and under such conditions they are bound to succeed."

If they did in Huns' Valley, much of the credit must go to George Doery. He seems to have been a natural leader, a fine organizer, and an excellent farmer and cattleman. Not the least of his achievements was that he acted as English teacher of his people. Under a man like this, the community made relatively quick progress and attracted settlers from elsewhere. Soon, as J. B. Hedges points out in his *Building the Canadian West*, they became quite a "heterogeneous flock, composed of Magyars, Slovaks, Ruthenians, Czechs and South Slavs." There is also good evidence that the Slovaks of the settlement were nationally conscious, and that they certainly did not allow the Magyars to lord it over them the way they did in the old country. How this was sometimes done is described in a report printed in the Sessional Papers of 1893: "The Huns and Sclavish [i.e. the Slavic people] had a nasty habit to fight among them with long-bladed knives."

The success of the Huns' Valley enterprise enhanced Esterhazy's standing in the eyes of the Canadian government, so much so that it granted a very substantial allowance for those times—$25,000—for a bigger movement of immigrants Esterhazy announced he was preparing. At first he spoke of 3,000 families, but in the end only thirty-five, again unemployed coal-miners from Pennsylvania with their women and children, set out in June 1886. This time the destination was the virgin lands north of the Qu'Appelle River in Assiniboia. Again the CPR helped with some initial assistance to the settlers. The climate, unfortunately, proved less benevolent: only eleven families were hardy enough to brave another winter. They were rewarded for their endurance by greatly improved conditions and the first signs that farming in Assiniboia might become quite a lucrative occupation. The community they built was named Esterhazy. It preserves to our

day the memory of the man who, spiritually at least, laid its foundations. The names which one can still read on the monument erected in
honour of the Esterhazy originals show that about half of them—Bab-
jak, Horniak, Sýkora, Smrekovský, Krupa, Lacko, and others—were
Slovaks, the other half Magyars.

An initial attempt to bring more settlers to Esterhazy failed because
of a disastrous fire in the settlement, and the provisions Esterhazy
made for placing the colonists elsewhere met with little success. From
then on, the CPR and Esterhazy parted company. Undaunted, the
latter brought out yet another two small expeditions in the spring of
1888. They contained for the first time direct immigrants from Hungary, mostly Magyars. One group settled at Neepawa, Manitoba, the
other founded the hamlet of Kaposvar. Its name, and that of Kaposvar
Creek, recall this last recorded effort of Esterhazy's to colonize the
Canadian west. But his settlements remained, and in due course
prospered. They, incidentally, also soon attracted Czech settlers.
There was, for instance, one Heindrich, a native of Domažlice in
Bohemia, who came to Esterhazy as early as 1888, and he was followed as time went on by a number of others.

At this point, we must interrupt our chronological account and go
back a few years to examine the question of who was the very first
Czech or Slovak to come to Canada as an immigrant. This is perhaps
of no great importance, but it does have some curiosity value. In any
case, there is no definite answer. There are only indications that they
may have been the Bellans, from Trenčín in Slovakia, with the head
of the family arriving in the early 1870s. At any rate, a son, Joseph
Bellan, came to Toronto as a thirteen-year-old lad in 1878, to join his
father. The Bellans are variously said to have owned a wirework
factory, a flower shop, and a pool room; and Joseph many years later
told a writing friend (Fero Zeman) that he had served for three years
in the militia and taken part in the Red River Expedition of 1885. No
Bellan can, however, be found in the nominal rolls of the force which
went out to crush the Riel Rebellion. The name that comes closest is
"J. Beldon," but even if it were a mis-spelling, it is not likely that
Beldon was in fact our Bellan, for he served in Steele's Scouts, an
irregular unit in which city men would hardly have been enrolled.

One runs into other difficulties, too, when one tries to trace the Bellans' story. Let us merely say, then, that they probably *were* the first and that they led an active life in and around Toronto even though they may not have done everything they have been credited with, and leave it at that. Some Slovaks may have settled just outside Fort William as early as 1880. The precise date cannot now be ascertained, but if they did, they would range next to the Bellans as the oldest settlers.

Slovak miners—and a little later, also a lesser number of Czech—first came to Canada at the same time as did the first farmers. In 1885, a group of them set out in ox-drawn wagons from Shelby, Montana, on a westward trek which after some two weeks brought them to the new coal mines of Lethbridge in the North-West Territories, now Alberta. They must have been a hardy lot, physically and morally, for not only did they overcome a great many initial difficulties but they also maintained their social coherence and pride of origin. The Lethbridge Slovak community has always been very active and still numbers some six hundred.

As successful as was this first mining settlement, so unsuccessful was the second. We have already mentioned Count Esterhazy's abortive attempt to bring more settlers to the Assiniboia colony which bore his name. This was in 1887. Trying to tide his people at least over the first prairie winter, Esterhazy arranged for the men to work for the Moore & Hunter Company, which operated a mine at Stair, Manitoba. This did not work out for either side. The Slovak miners were dissatisfied with the labour and living conditions, and apparently said so. Their employers drew the easy conclusion which was standard in the harsh days of budding industrialization. "There seemed to be strong socialistic elements among the miners," it says in a letter from the owners which can be found in the Sessional Papers of 1887, "that are not at all desirable in the country." Needless to say, there is no evidence that the Slovaks of Stair were politically motivated in any way; they were just unhappy.

A bigger group of Slovak miners, over one hundred strong, came in 1898 from Pennsylvania, to work in the anthracite mines near Crow's Nest Camp, British Columbia, soon to be renamed Fernie after the traveller and prospector who discovered that western bonanza. And that it was, fabulous in its riches and its growth. The "Crow's Nest Coal Company" started operations in July 1898, at a location which up to then had been just wilderness. A year later, production stood at 116,000 tons of coal and 30,000 tons of coke a year, and the next at 220,000 tons and 74,000 tons, respectively. In 1902, the four-year-old mining town of Fernie had some 3,000 inhabitants. (Such facts help to show us why and how Canada was becoming around 1900 the promised land to European emigrants.)

In Fernie, also, occurred the first major catastrophe to befall the still tiny Czech and Slovak community in Canada. On May 12, 1902, there was an explosion in Colliery no. 2. In it perished the shift that was underground at the time, as well as the first rescue crew to respond to the alarm—over 150 men all told. At least eighteen of them were Slovaks, many natives of the Orava region. In fact, the last body to be recovered—a full two years after the tragedy—was that of a man identified by the receipt portion of a money order he carried in his wallet. The order was addressed to his family in far-off Liesek, in Slovak Upper Hungary.

There were Slovak miners at that time in other localities in the Rocky Mountains—in Derby, British Columbia, for instance, and in Bellevue and Frank, North-West Territories. At the latter place they worked for the "Canadian-American Coal and Coke Company," and were struck by yet another elemental catastrophe. Before five o'clock on the morning of April 29, 1903, Turtle Mountain, which towered above the mining settlement, literally split in half. An estimated seventy million tons of rock slid down the slope, to bury 3,200 acres of the valley beneath. Yet only some sixty people were killed; some were saved as if by a miracle. There was just a skeleton crew of seventeen underground at the time of the landslide, and it included eight "Sclaves," Poles, Slovaks, and Czechs. Only one of them perished, John Sirota from Orava—on his last day of work before returning to his homeland.

All in all, then, a beginning had been made with Czech and Slovak settlement in Canada, but by the end of the nineteenth century it was still only a beginning, and a very small one at that: some farm communities in the prairies, groups of miners in a few camps in the Rocky Mountains, no more. This was because in those years Canada was not an immigrants' country (at any rate, not one to tempt continental European immigrants) and the almost empty Canadian west even less so. In fact, in the late eighties and early nineties of the century immigration was very slow. In 1896, only 16,835 people came to this country to settle, fewer than in any other year since Confederation.

The great change occurred in that same year, 1896. A new and vigorous administration came into power, under Sir Wilfrid Laurier as prime minister. His minister of the interior, who was in charge of immigration, was Clifford Sifton, a former attorney-general of Manitoba, and an enthusiastic proponent of settlement and development in the Canadian west. On the books, of course, there were no serious impediments to immigration even before Sifton's times. Only three classes of persons were debarred from entry, the diseased, the criminal or vicious, and those likely to become public charges. But if there were no legal obstacles to speak of, the economic obstacles to immigration were formidable. In fact, they were such that, once an initial outburst of zeal and energy in the early eighties was spent, the authorities became so discouraged as to give up recruiting settlers.

All this changed under Laurier and Sifton. As the terms of world trade turned in favour of Canada, unprecedented efforts were made to procure the human material necessary for the full realization of the country's potential. "The federal government plunged into a systematic campaign of publicity," Donald Creighton recounts in his *Dominion of the North*, "with advertisements in thousands of papers, immigration agents everywhere on two continents, and great excursion trainloads of pressmen and farmers to behold the wonders of the 'last, best west.'" Immigration figures mounted quickly, to 55,747 in 1901 and to 211,653 in 1906.

Czech and Slovak settlement had a share, though admittedly quite modest, in the immigration boom. As our settlers were listed as "Austrians" and "Hungarians" respectively in the censuses of the time, it is difficult to determine with any degree of accuracy what their numbers were. An educated guess is that at the time of the 1901 census there were about a thousand Czechs and Slovaks in Canada, and anywhere between three and four thousand in the 1911 census year. A guide to the latter figure is the fact that about 1,800 Canadian residents were then listed as born in Bohemia and Moravia. Probably the great majority of them were racially Czechs. It is more difficult, however, to determine the number of Slovaks, but it seems certain that they were more numerous in Canada than the Czechs. Thus, a figure of 3,500 by 1911 does not appear unreasonable.

The majority of those Czechs and Slovaks who came before the First World War were still farmers and miners, and they were still as a rule recruited by colonization agents, mostly of the CPR. (It is an indication of the growing importance of the Czechs and Slovaks as settlers that one of their nationality, George Zeman, was at that time hired by the CPR as one of its agents.) The Slovaks continued to come mostly by way of the United States, although direct immigration from Europe was starting as well. The Czechs came from their homeland, but also from among the colonists who had earlier tried settling in Russian-Polish Volhynia. Thus Volhynian Czechs in 1898 founded Gerald, not far from Esterhazy in Assiniboia. Others joined budding farm communities in the same area, Hanley, Broderick, Milden, Strongfield, Kenaston. Czechs and Slovaks from the United States settled around 1900 in Marriott, Valley Centre, and Glenside in the same general region. The first Czech, John Nenička, to come to Rat Portage (now Kenora) on the Lake of the Woods, Ontario, arrived in 1896, and the first Slovak, Charles Šáňa, arrived there four years later.

Even a place named Prague was founded (in 1904) near Viking, in what one year later became the province of Alberta. The founding fathers, though, did not come from the ancient *caput regni*, the "city of the hundred spires," but from Prague, Oklahoma. Among them was Joseph Hájek, who had previously farmed in Nebraska, and later became the first "homespun" archivist of the Czechs in western Canada. There was also some settlement motivated by religion, at any rate at the outset. Thus, between 1910 and 1912, families from Moravia took up land among the Mennonites, around Morden in southern Manitoba. In the far north-west of the same province, in the Swan

River region, Czech and Slovak Baptists settled in the neighbourhood of Minitonas.

More Czechs and Slovaks also came to work in the Alberta mines, at Evergreen, Coleman, and Blairmore. The last of these mining towns has the distinction of being the place where, as early as 1910, the first Czech or Slovak newspaper in Canada was published, George Kleskeň's *Slovenské Slovo* ("Slovak Word"). We shall have more to tell about it in Chapter Three. The gold mines of northern Ontario also attracted Czech and Slovak workmen, who soon were much in evidence around Kirkland Lake and Haileybury, in particular in the "tent villages" of Pike Lake and Homestead. The community in Fort William, Ontario, too, which soon became a very important one, had its origin in mining activities, even if indirectly. It was at the coal docks of the great inland port that Slovak workers found jobs in the early days. There, near the waterfront, also stands their old Church of Saints Peter and Paul, erected in 1911, during the pastorate of Father Francis Maynard, SJ, who, though French, learned to speak Slovak in order to properly serve his flock.

Finally, there were the first, tentative beginnings of urban settlement. Otto Ház came to Kingston, Ontario, in 1898 and founded Canada Vinegar Ltd., a concern which soon prospered. In 1900, four Czech families took up residence in Edmonton, the future capital of Alberta. Skilled Czech mechanics arrived in Windsor, Ontario, to work for the Ford Motor Company. The odd Czech and Slovak turned up in Toronto, albeit more often as not as a transient.

The most significant urban settlement of the Czech and Slovak group, however, developed in Winnipeg, Manitoba. It was predominantly Czech, and its founding father probably was Wenceslas Halama who came in 1895, in the service of the Archbishop of St. Boniface. He was soon joined by his brother Anthony and his brother-in-law Frank Blahník, with their families. Up to then, a fair number of Czechs and Slovaks had passed through Winnipeg on their way to the virgin farmlands farther west. They had stopped, bought supplies, and moved on. Now Czechs began to come to stay. They worked on the railroad and in the construction trades; they were independent artisans and businessmen. Among the early leaders of the growing community there were such as Joseph Adámek, Jacob Veselák, Wenceslas Pátek, Wenceslas Moravec, Louis Louch, Jacob Hrabí. The most remarkable among them was probably Frank Dojáček. Businessman, community organizer, philanthropist, churchman, he started by selling bibles on Manitoba farms and ended up the most successful ethnic publisher in western Canada.

From the beginning, the Winnipeg community was closely knit and nationally highly conscious. By 1913, a Czecho-Slav Benevolent Association was formed in Winnipeg, the first independent socio-economic organization in the ethnic group. And when the First World War started, Winnipeg was the focal point for the group's war effort, which, considering its size, was very significant.

There were a fair number of Czechs and Slovaks in the Canadian armed forces of the First World War. They enlisted where opportunity offered, but in Winnipeg they did so *en masse*, in the "Bohemian Detachment" of the 223rd Battalion, Canadian Expeditionary Force. The 223rd assumed the name of "Canadian Scandinavians," and its cap badge showed the somewhat morose face of a Viking warrior, with drooping moustaches and a horned helmet. The idea for unit, name, and badge came from the Manitoba Scandinavian community, and many of the battalion's officers were of Scandinavian extraction. The "other ranks," though, came from every hue of the rainbow of nationalities which peopled the Canadian prairies.

We read in Militia Orders 1917 that the 223rd embarked at Halifax, Nova Scotia, in the troop transport SS *Justicia*, on May 3, 1917. The officer commanding was Major Hannes Marino Hanneson, an Icelander. The nominal roll shows seventy-six men who gave "Bohemia" as their homeland. A few of them were old soldiers: under "former unit" we find "U.S. Army" (from which came the two most senior men, Sergeant Joseph Frank Musil and Lance/Sergeant Frank Klepal), "Bohemian Army," and in one case, that of Lance/Corporal Joseph Bondy, who appears to have been a one-time Foreign Legionnaire, "French Army." "Bohemian Army" was, of course, a piece of fiction. There was none, but at this time it was no doubt thought inappropriate to put in "Austro-Hungarian Army" after the names of those who had done their stretch of compulsory service in the old homeland. So, as a way out of the dilemma, an army was revived on paper which had not existed in reality for almost three hundred years. Some of the men of the "Bohemian Detachment" had crossed over from the neutral United States to enlist in Canada. The majority came from every known Canadian habitat of the ethnic group, from Esterhazy and Evergreen to Edmonton and Winnipeg.

The 223rd never fought as a unit, but upon arrival in France was absorbed in the 11th Reserve Battalion of the Canadian Corps. Its members were assigned as replacements to a number of Canadian formations. They had come too late for the Battle of Vimy, but in good time for the even worse ordeal of Passchendaele. We may suppose that the men of what had been the "Bohemian Detachment" of the "Canadian Scandinavians"—this curious combination is in itself an indication of the direction Canadian nation-building was then beginning to take—fought with half their hearts filled with loyalty to their new homeland and half with the desire to win a better future for their old.

With the First World War, the pioneer days were over for the Czech and Slovak settlement in Canada. It numbered now an estimated 6,000, and was nearing the day when it would make a mark on its environment. Beyond that, still very far off but perhaps already discernible as a faint gleam on the Canadian horizon, lay the fulfilment of the prediction Watson Kirkconnell was later to make in his *Canada, Europe and Hitler*: "All the values of civilization are not summed up in the Anglo-Saxon. To weave into the Canadian fabric the multicoloured threads of all Europe's cultural legacies ought, if it were possible, to produce in the end a civilization of unusual richness. In the ancient Greek world, it was Athens, the most miscegenated in blood and culture, that led in all artistic and cultural achievements." A Canadian culture that would be a composite of all the best western man has produced is a lofty ideal, a dream perhaps, but an objective towards which, consciously or unconsciously, all the nationalities which make up "the Canadian mosaic" have been working.

THE ERA OF
MASS IMMIGRATION
(from 1918)

About 6,000 Czechs and Slovaks in Canada at the end of the First World War—not much to show for something like thirty-five years of more or less planned (on the part of the immigrants and on the part of the authorities) settlement. The reason for such a meagre result was, of course, the greater attractiveness of the neighbouring United States. It was not all a matter of economics; emotion played a role, too.

The pre-1914 Czech and Slovak immigrant from Austria-Hungary sought a home beyond the Atlantic both because it promised a better material life and because it meant deliverance from the stifling atmosphere of bureaucratic oppression—or at least bureaucratic authoritarianism—to which the small man was exposed in the old country. That pressure exercised by petty officialdom in helmets or peaked caps, threadbare but buoyed by the sense of being in authority, was associated in the minds of Czech and Slovak emigrants with the monarchic system and the privileged classes that derived their positions and power from that system. Simple people—and as we said earlier, the Czechs and Slovaks who came to North America before the First World War were predominantly farm labourers, industrial workers, small artisans—could not associate liberty with life under a monarchy. They believed that they would find freedom, political, economic, personal, in the republican United States rather than in the Dominion of Canada ruled by a king emperor. The concept of a sovereign who does not govern was too complicated for them to understand.

The more thoughtful among the prospective immigrants to North America were also dissuaded from choosing Canada as the country in which to settle by a Canadian immigration policy which gave preference to people from the British Isles. This was clearly shown in the Immigration Act of 1910, and successive ministers charged with administering it certainly did not conceal the fact. Not that Slavic immigrants were in any way officially discriminated against; it was simply that those whose mother tongue was English were considered the most desirable. After all, even immigrants from France were put into the favoured posiiton enjoyed by settlers from Britain and the United States only in 1949. In the old empire based on "kingship and kinship," the "kin" was British. As to the rest, it was up to them to see how, as it were, they might marry into the family.

It should be repeated here, to avoid misunderstanding, that actual immigration practice was liberal and benevolent. Also before the First World War Canada was a good country for non-British people in which to settle. But it was no melting pot like the United States. The promise, explicit if often illusory, of short-order Americanization that comforted the anguished immigrant to the United States as soon as he set foot on the pier, was missing in Canada. Not many concessions—some would say none at all—were at that time made to alien outlooks and habits. No wonder, then, that the non-British immigrant generally felt at home more quickly in the more diffuse and cosmopolitan society of the United States. The benefits of a policy of integration of immigrants as it developed in Canada, compared to the American one of assimilation, became apparent only much later.

The trend towards settlement in the United States would probably have continued, had not the latter, soon after the First World War, slammed the door in the face of most European immigrants except the so-called Nordic ones. This is not the place to discuss in any detail the United States quota system except to say that successive legislation ultimately restricted Czech and Slovak (and, of course, all other eastern and southern European) immigration to so low a figure that it became totally insignificant. Thus, the Act of 1921 limited the number of immigrants of any one nationality to a yearly 3 per cent of the foreign-born residents of that nationality as shown by the census of 1910. The Act of 1924 lowered this to 2 per cent according to the census of 1890. Finally, in 1929, the national origin plan was put into effect. Basically, it worked—and with some modifications and simplifications, still works—this way: The ethnic composition of the population of the United States is determined from current census figures. Each national group is then allocated a proportion of a maximum yearly immigration figure of 150,000 equal to its ratio of the total population. This is "the quota."

The immediate result of the introduction of the quota system was that immigration to the United States that had reached one million a year before the First World War, fell to one-tenth that number—the much restricted, admissible total was not even reached, because the comparatively large quotas allocated to north-western Europe were usually not filled. Where people from other parts of Europe had made up 80 per cent of the inflow in the immediate pre-war years, they now comprised less than 15 per cent of the total. As to the Czechoslovak quota, it was 3,073 a year under the Act of 1924, a mere fraction of the number who formerly migrated yearly to the United States. The figure is interesting also for another reason: it shows that there must have been upwards of 150,000 Czechs and Slovaks (precisely how many cannot be determined, since they were, then, generally counted among the Austrians and Hungarians) in the United States by 1890. In Canada there were at that time only a few hundred.

This digression into the development of American immigration policies was necessary to explain the sudden upswing in Czech and Slovak immigration to Canada in the years after the First World War. It would have been even greater had the inclination to emigrate been as strong after the First World War as before it. However, the forces working for emigration from the new Czechoslovakia were offset by others, even more cogent, against it. Among the former, the most compelling was the experience of the war. People who had lived through the slaughter at the fronts and through the hunger at home may have been excused if they had written off the old Europe and the spirit that produced it as beyond redemption, and had wished to put between it and themselves as great a distance as possible. Many did just that. On the other hand, the Czechs and Slovaks had a new state of their own, democratic, liberal, socially progressive. With stocks of almost everything exhausted by the war, the economy was active and employment plentiful. A far-sighted land reform offered ownership of the soil to many former farm labourers, from whose ranks had come the majority of those who had sought their fortune beyond the Atlantic. All in all, the motives for staying at home were the stronger. If the number of Czechs and Slovaks in Canada more than tripled between the census of 1921 and 1931, from 8,840 to 30,401, it was because Canada was now the emigrants' promised land, just as the United States had been in earlier years.

Progressively, though, as post-war transportation difficulties diminished and exaggerated hopes of universal contentment and prosperity in the home country dissipated, emigration from Czechoslovakia increased. In part, this was also due to too much centralization which did not go down well in Slovakia. But, whatever the reasons, steadily rising numbers of Czechs and Slovaks entered Canada in the twenties. Thus, whereas just over 2,000 Czechs and Slovaks came to this country in 1923, more than 7,000 did in 1928. Throughout this period, there were among the immigrants five Slovaks for every one Czech.

The Slovak settlers at that time were still in their overwhelming majority farm workers. As a rule, they had made their contacts through the agents of the big railway companies, the Canadian Pacific and later also the Canadian National, and were directed by them mostly to the Canadian West. Yet, if the method of settlement was not very different from that common before the First World War, the type of settler most certainly was. The forerunners, those who had come prior to the war, were in great part poorly educated—as we have seen, the schools in Slovak Upper Hungary taught in Hungarian and there was little inclination on the part of the Slovaks to frequent them and just as little on the part of the Magyar authorities to enforce Slovak education. There was among them no habit of political activity, and national consciousness, though strong, was entirely emotional. The post-war settlers were quite a different breed. Mostly young, they had benefited from the Republic's school system, with Slovak naturally the language of instruction, and in many respects also from their compulsory service in the army. They had had a taste of political life, particularly vigorous and unshackled at the village level, yet many had been left behind, economically. Thus there was a go-getting spirit in many of them which had been rare among their countrymen who had come to Canada earlier. Not surprisingly then, it was this wave of immigrants who founded the fraternal organizations and the communal enterprises of the ethnic group, many of which have lasted to the present day.

These relatively well-equipped post-1914 Slovak immigrants also fared better economically than their predecessors. Farm wages in the late twenties were fairly good considering the price levels, and they became better the farther west a man went. A Slovak farmhand—there were comparatively few Czechs among these general agricultural workers—could count on earning around 40 dollars a month during the growing season, besides his free lodgings and food. In the winter, if he did not want to stay on the farm doing chores for his keep, he usually found work elsewhere, in the prairie towns, in the forests, on road construction. It was not an easy life, but for most it was reasonably secure.

Slovak settlers spread all over the west, with perhaps a slight preference for Manitoba. They had a kind of guardian angel, there, in Peter Sherman, Sr., who was their interpreter and employment agent, their adviser, and even their host in the occasional emergency. The Canadian National Railway was vigorously encouraging colonization in the Minitonas district, where, as we have seen, some Czechs and Slovaks had already settled before the war and where even today 60 per cent of the people are of central European descent. Soon the newcomers formed a substantial part of the populations of such prairie communities as Oak Bluff, Sanford, Dugald, Elm Grove, and Rosewood. Not all of the Slovak immigrants of the period, of course, were farmers. There were among them miners and factory workers, and a number ended up in the forest industry of British Columbia.

As already pointed out, not many new Czech immigrants came to the farms of western Canada. There was, however, at least one notable exception: sugarbeet growing became something of a Czech preserve. The Sugar Beet Growers' Association of Canada had arranged with the Czechoslovak Overseas Institute (the word "zahraniční," literally "beyond the frontiers," is translated here as "overseas," although the Institute also looked after Czechoslovak interests in European countries) for the settlement in Canada of farmers with experience in the growing of this produce. Many of them came from Moravia, and they concentrated in Alberta, around Lethbridge, in such places as Raymond, Barnwell, and Cranford. With the encouragement of their employers a number of them soon managed to buy their own farms. This, at the time, was not too difficult: a quarter section of good land cost anywhere between 4,000 and 5,000 dollars, including the essential equipment, and 1,000 dollars was a sufficient down-payment. A hard and frugal sugarbeet grower could save that much in a relatively short time, working on the land in the spring and autumn seasons, and earning money elsewhere in the summer and winter.

It was also sugarbeet that brought a larger group of Czechs and Slovaks to Southern Ontario. Attracted by advantageous offers made by the CPR, most of them settled in a thirty-mile radius around the city of Chatham. After a while, a good many changed from sugarbeet to tobacco growing and market gardening. It was this group which formed the nucleus of the particularly active national group in Chatham.

Most of the Czech immigrants, and a smaller proportion of the Slovak, preferred to settle in the cities as industrial workers and artisans. There had been no larger-scale Czech and Slovak urban settlements before that, except those already mentioned in Winnipeg and Fort William. Now small communities grew up wherever a pair of skilled hands was needed. How quickly they grew can be shown by the example of Toronto, where the Czech and Slovak community numbered just thirty souls in 1923, but around 2,500 ten years later. In Montreal, the growth was even more spectacular: hardly any Czech and Slovak residents at the census time of 1921, and 3,643 according to the 1931 census. Montreal, incidentally, boasted the biggest Czech and Slovak community in Canada until the end of the Second World War, when it was overtaken, and then gradually outdistanced, by Toronto. In the twenties, significant groups of Czech and Slovak settlers also came to other Canadian industrial cities—to Windsor and Oshawa where they were attracted by the expanding automotive industry, to Hamilton and Vancouver. Whereas in 1921 about 65 per cent or 5,724 of the 8,840 Czechs and Slovaks in Canada lived on the land, the proportion was only 14,705 out of 30,401 in 1931—less than one-half. With this progressive "urbanization," there also began a gradual change in the relative strength of Czechs and Slovaks in this country. The former were starting to catch up in numbers, even though they never did reach parity.

The two most significant characteristics of the wave of Czech and

Slovak immigrants who entered Canada between the First World War and the Great Depression were, first, that it was still what may be called (without any derogatory connotation) a proletarian immigration, generally of agricultural and industrial labourers, with a leavening of skilled manual workers, but only a very small intellectual group; and second, that it had already shown a remarkable capacity for integration into Canadian life. Even though learning English or French did not come easily as a rule to persons with limited education, the Czechs and Slovaks in Canada always managed to stay out of the ethnic ghettos. There are a number of yardsticks by which to measure this propensity for integration. One of them is the rate of intermarriage. Here, a study undertaken in 1931 by the Social Service Council of the United Church of Canada showed that 9.6 per cent of Czech and Slovak men and 11.3 per cent of Czech and Slovak women in Canada married into British stock. This put the men into third place among immigrants from central, eastern, and southern Europe (behind the Greeks and the Italians), and the women into first place. By comparison, the intermarriage rate with British-stock Canadians of the Ukrainians, for instance, was .7 per cent for their men and .4 per cent for their women.

The Great Depression put a virtual stop to Czech and Slovak immigration to Canada, just as it did to the whole thirty-five-year-old scheme of officially encouraged and supported immigration. Nothing had shown the purpose of immigration more clearly than the fact that its administration came under the Department of Mines and Resources; a separate ministry was only established in 1950. Immigrants were indeed an all-important economic resource in a developing country, to be sought energetically when required. Just as naturally, the tap was turned off when there was no need. This was the easier as, in contrast to the situation in the United States, admission to Canada had always been more or less discretionary (though not arbitrary), dependent on the immigrants' desirability from the aspect of the "climatic, industrial, social, educational, labour or other conditions or requirements of Canada." During the depression, then, emigration from Czechoslovakia was on a rising scale, but the emigrants, apart from some exceptions, did not get to Canada.

The experiences of the Great Depression have been described so often that it will not be necessary to linger over them here. By and large, the Czechs and Slovaks in Canada got through this trying period better than most, no doubt mainly because one-half of them were still rural settlers. This clearly accounts for the temporary reversal of the natural, in a growing industrial country, trend from the land to the town. Whereas according to the 1931 census, 48.37 per cent of the persons of Czech and Slovak origin lived in rural communities, the ratio was 52.83 per cent at the census time of 1941. In the cities, of course, the Czech and Slovak industrial worker or artisan had as tough a time keeping body and soul together as the next man.

About the work performed by the Czech and Slovak Canadians during the Second World War we shall hear in the next chapter. Here, in the historical context, there is not much to be said about the period. The fact that immigration was virtually halted during the war years resulted in there being only very few newcomers to the country. Also, the stern experiences of the Great Depression, shared materially and emotionally with all other Canadians, had, if anything, speeded the process of integration. Consequently, the great majority of Czechs and Slovaks who wished to enlist simply went to the nearest recruiting office of one of the three Canadian armed services. They were then spread as individuals through many units and naval vessels. The predominantly Czech and Slovak unit of the Reserve Army at the Bata Shoe Company at Batawa, Ontario, was thus an exception to the rule. At the beginning of the war, the honorary consul of Czechoslovakia in Toronto, Horace H. Van Wart, QC, did invaluable work in encouraging and counselling Czechs and Slovaks flocking to the Canadian colours. This was particularly important in the first months of the conflict when offers of service by far outdistanced the absorptive capacities of the Canadian armed services. One of the authors of this book is among the many indebted to Mr. Van Wart for getting him into a Canadian uniform. Later in the war, a Czechoslovak military mission also recruited Czechs and Slovaks in Canada for the Czechoslovak army-in-exile, but by then most of those eligible and eager to serve had already joined the colours. As to their performance, no more need be said than that it is part of the proud fighting record of the

Royal Canadian Navy, the Canadian Army, and the Royal Canadian
Air Force in the Second World War.

We have now to return to the year 1938, which in a way is a
turning-point in the history of Czech and Slovak immigration to
Canada. In the half-century before that, most immigrants were economically motivated in their decision to come to Canada, and the
overwhelming majority of them were "blue-collar" workers. From
then on, their reasons tended to be political—they were looking for a
refuge—and the majority were in the white-collar category. A learned
enquiry, Anthony H. Richmond's *Post-War Immigrants in Canada*,
even though not concerned with the first influx of refugees from
Nazism, shows the change in facts and figures. Two sets should be
sufficient to make the point: For 72.9 per cent of the eastern Europeans who came to Canada between 1946 and 1961, politics was the
motive for migration; it was so for only 3.2 per cent of the immigrants
from the British Isles. Of the eastern Europeans, 75.9 per cent arrived
with their minds already made up to stay in Canada permanently; the
corresponding ratios were 35.4 per cent for immigrants from the
United Kingdom, and 30 per cent for "other English-speaking" newcomers. The proportion of persons with university education was
uncommonly high among the new immigrants from eastern Europe,
whereas it had been minuscule among their predecessors before 1938.
   Compared with figures from other nationalities, the number of
Czechs and Slovaks who came to Canada as fugitives from Nazism
was relatively small. This is understandable when one considers that
up to late 1938 the Czechs and Slovaks generally believed that the
German threat would be met, by armed resistance if necessary. The
shock of the Munich surrender was the greater since hardly anybody
expected it. After Munich, not much time remained to leave the country, nor was there any legal possibility of transferring abroad the financial means, in convertible currency, which at that time an immigrant
was required to possess upon entry into Canada. And after the occupation of the rest of Czechoslovakia in March 1939, the borders of the
unfortunate country shut tight, letting through only the occasional adventurous escapee.

The influx into Canada of Czech and Slovak refugees from communism, which began with the Prague coup in late February 1948, was much greater. Before that, in 1946 and 1947, a limited number of supporters of the wartime Slovak State had entered Canada under the title of "displaced persons." Had the Immigration Act of 1952 been in force then, they would have been ineligible, and technically they were probably so before that—the Slovak State, after all, had been a dictatorship, associated with the national-socialist and fascist dictatorships in Germany and Italy, and it had been at war with the Allies. The Department of Immigration's discretionary powers were, however, exercised—no doubt for humanitarian reasons—in favour of this group of Slovak refugees. This was in keeping with the general, praiseworthy liberality displayed by Canada where the admission of post-war European refugees was concerned. Altogether more than 300,000 have been made welcome in this country since 1946. This is not much less than in the United States, which has ten times the population of Canada but which has special statutory provisions for regulating immigration quantitatively. The Czech and Slovak refugees from communism are of all classes; they come from among the students, professional and business men, artists, manual workers of all descriptions.

After the spring of 1948, it became increasingly difficult to flee from Czechoslovakia. The Iron Curtain came down quickly, in the physical sense, with the construction of elaborate systems of frontier barriers. In the case of Czechoslovakia it proved well-nigh unbreakable. Immigration into Canada of Czechs and Slovaks soon diminished to a mere trickle, something like one hundred a year. It has picked up somewhat only quite recently as a result of the more liberal (compared with those of the fifties and the early sixties) policies of the Czechoslovak regime. The latter now allows the emigration of a certain number of older people anxious to join their families in Canada. Perhaps more important, travel to the free west is now (1967) somewhat less restricted for Czechoslovak citizens, and this enables some of the travellers to defect. The actual numbers are still very small, but they are rising. In 1966, they were around thirty a month in the first half of the year, and between forty-five and fifty a month in the second half.

Almost all the political refugees of the period from 1938 onwards settled in the cities. Ontario, and in particular Toronto, was, at least initially, the goal of the majority. In a way, they had it easier than their predecessors, and in a way more difficult. They came to a developed country experiencing its most rapid industrial growth, and thus in need of skills of all kinds. The rough-and-ready pioneer days lay far behind. There was already leisure and a climate of appreciation for artistic values. A comprehensive system of social legislation was removing the old dangers of economic ups and downs which used to hang over the individual in earlier days. On the other hand, the ties with the past of the political refugee are more complex and restricting than those binding the immigrant who simply came to find a piece of land of his own or a better wage. While it was often difficult for the old-time immigrant to gain a material foothold in the country, it was just as often difficult for the post-1938 immigrant to gain a psychological one.

Even so, the more recent Czech and Slovak immigrants have also integrated themselves successfully into Canadian life. The overwhelming majority of them have done well in their various callings. They have founded industries and businesses, established themselves in the professions and the art world, acquired farms, and found their places as wage-earners. Later on we will see just how well some of them performed. As to mental integration, the fact that Canada is still not a melting pot in which newcomers are assimilated to a native pattern (as in the United States) may have deterred early immigrants who saw in it a device for keeping the non-Anglo-Saxons apart, as second-class citizens in fact, though not in law. Experience, however, has shown that the Canadian emphasis on integration rather than assimilation, on the creation of a multi-cultural rather than a mono-cultural society, is attractive to newcomers, and helps them find their bearings and feel at home in this country. "A Canadian citizen is privileged," says a citizenship program circular issued some time ago in Vancouver, "to live in a land where he is not only allowed but also encouraged to perpetuate the language, religion, and culture of his forebears."

Under such favourable conditions, more than 80,000 people of

Czech and Slovak origin now live in Canada. The precise number at the time of the census of 1961 was 73,061, of which about one-half, 35,743 to be exact, were actually born in Czechoslovakia or in parts of old Austria-Hungary that later became Czechoslovakia. Our estimate takes into account the natural population growth and what little Czech and Slovak immigration there was in the intervening six years. Although the precise proportion of Czechs and Slovaks is difficult to ascertain—the census does not make a distinction—a safe estimate would be that, in Canada, the Slovaks now outnumber their Czech brethren by about two to one. The Czechs and Slovaks thus do not form one of the large ethnic groups in this country, but they are appreciable in numbers, and, as the next two chapters should show, even more so in their share in Canadian life especially in the economic and the cultural fields.

Bibliography

Almanacs, Canadian Slovak League, for the years 1953, 1955, 1959, 1960, Winnipeg, Man., Toronto.

ANGUS, H. F., "The Future of Immigration into Canada," *Canadian Journal of Economics and Political Science*, 12 (Aug. 1946).

BOUSCAREU, ANTHONY T., *International Migrations since 1945*, New York, 1963.

BROWN, G. W., (ed.), *Canada*, United Nations Series, R. J. Kerner (ed.), Berkeley, Calif., Toronto, 1950.

BROWN, W. H., *The Slovakian Community in Montreal* (unpubl. thesis, Dept. of Sociology, McGill Univ., Montreal, 1927).

Canada Year Books, Ottawa, Dominion Bureau of Statistics, annually or biennally since 1905.

ČAPEK, THOMAS, *The Čechs (Bohemians) in America*, New York, Boston, 1920.

Citizenship, Immigration and Ethnic Groups in Canada, a bibliography of research, publ. and unpubl. sources, 1920–1958, Canada, Dept. of Citizenship and Immigration, Ottawa, 1961.

CORBETT, DAVID C., *Canada's Immigration Policy: A Critique*, Toronto, 1957.

—— "Immigration and Economic Development," *Canadian Journal of Economics and Political Science*, 17 (1951).

CORBETT, JULIAN S., *England in the Seven Years' War*, London, 1907.

CORMIE, JOHN A., *Canada and The New Canadians*, Social Service Council, United Church of Canada, Winnipeg, Toronto, 1931.

CREIGHTON, DONALD, *Dominion of The North*, Toronto, 1957.

CRESSWELL, H. C. P., *The Canadian Pacific and Immigration*, Canadian Pacific Railway Company, Montreal.

CULLITON, J. T., *Assisted Emigration and Land Settlement*, McGill University Economic Studies, no. 9, Montreal, 1927.

DAWSON, C. A., *Group Settlement: Ethnic Communities in Western Canada*, Series of Canadian Frontiers of Settlement, vol. VII, Toronto, 1936.

DENIS, E., and J. VANČURA, *Čechy po Bílé Hoře* ("The Czech Lands after the Battle at the White Mountain"), part I., vol. II., (Czech transl. of French original), Prague, 1905.

DRÁBEK, JAROSLAV, *Čtení o Moravských Bratřích* ("Readings on the Moravian Brethren"), New York, 1962.

EGGLESTON, WILFRID, *The Road to Nationhood*, Oxford, 1946.

Encyclopaedia Britannica, vol. XX, "Seven Years' War," Chicago, London, Toronto, 1959.

ENGLAND, ROBERT, *The Central European Immigrant in Canada*, Toronto, 1929.

FOWKE, V. C., *Canadian Agricultural Policy: The Historical Pattern*, Toronto, 1947.

GIBBON, JOHN MURRAY, *Canadian Mosaic, The Making of a Northern Nation*, Toronto, 1938.

—— *The New Canadian Loyalists*, Toronto, 1941.

GRAY, ELMA E., *Wilderness Christians: The Moravian Mission to the Delaware Indians*, Toronto, 1956.

GUILLET, EDWIN and MARY, *The Pathfinders of North America*, Toronto, 1957.

HAMILTON, JOHN TAYLOR, *The History of the Church known as The Moravian Church, 1859*, Bethlehem, Pa., 1900.

HANSEN, M. L., *The Mingling of the Canadian and American Peoples*, The Relations of Canada and the United States Series, New Haven, Toronto, 1940.

HEDGES, J. B., *Building the Canadian West*, New York, 1939.

HRUBY, JIŘÍ G., "Immigration des Tchèques et des Slovaques au Canada," (unpubl. thesis, University of Montreal, 1954).

HUTTON, J. E., *A History of Moravian Missions*, Moravian Publications Office, London, Dublin, 1922.

INNIS, H. A., *A History of the Canadian Pacific Railway*, Toronto, 1923.

—— "Settlement and The Mining Frontier," W. A. MACKINTOSH, and W. L. G. JOERG, (eds.), *Canadian Frontiers of Settlement*, part II, vol. IX, Toronto, 1936.

INNIS, M. Q., *An Economic History of Canada* (rev. ed.), Toronto, 1943.

ISAAC, J., *The Economics of Migration*, London, 1947.

KAGE, JOSEPH, *With Faith and Thanksgiving: The Story of Two Hundred Years of Jewish Immigration and Immigrant Aid Effort in Canada (1760–1960)*, Montreal, 1962.

KAYE, V. J., "Canadians of Slovak Origin. A Brief Survey," *Canadian Slavonic Papers*, 4 (1959).

KIRKCONNELL, WATSON, *Canada, Europe and Hitler*, Toronto, 1939.

—— *Canadians All*, issued by the Director of Public Information under authority of the Minister of National War Services, Ottawa, June 1941.

LA TROBE, BENJAMIN, *With The Harmony to Labrador: Notes of a visit to the Moravian Mission Stations on the North-East Coast of Labrador*, Moravian Church and Mission Agency, London, 1888.

Lower, A. R. M., "Settlement and the Forest Frontier," W. A. Mackintosh, and W. L. G. Joerg, (eds.), *Canadian Frontiers of Settlement*, part II, vol. IX, Toronto, 1936.

Mackintosh, W. A., "Canada as an Area for Settlement," Isaiah Bowman, (ed.), *Limits of Land Settlement*, Council on Foreign Relations, New York, 1937.

—— "Prairie Settlement: the Geographic Setting," W. A. Mackintosh, and W. L. G. Joerg, (ed.), *Canadian Frontiers of Settlement*, Toronto, 1934.

Murin, J. J., La naissance et l'évolution de l'émigration slovaque (unpubl. thesis, University of Montreal, 1953).

Origin, Birthplace, Nationality and Language of the Canadian People (a Census study based on the Census of 1921 and supplementary data), Dominion Bureau of Statistics, Ottawa, 1929.

Památník ("A Memorial") of the 50 Years' Anniversary, Canadian Czechoslovak Benevolent Association, Winnipeg, Man., 1963.

Památník ("A Memorial"), Czechoslovak National Alliance in Canada, Winnipeg, Man., 1943.

Parkman, Francis, *Montcalm and Wolfe*, Boston, 1884.

Parrott, Cecil, "Great Moravia's Dark Age Culture," *The Illustrated London News*, Dec. 17, 1966.

Porter, John, *The Vertical Mosaic: An Analysis of Social Class and Power in Canada*, Toronto, 1965.

Quinn, D. B., *The Voyages & Colonizing Enterprises of Sir Humphrey Gilbert*, London: Hakluyk Society, 1940.

Rekem, J., *Souvenir Book* (to the Fifth Anniversary of the Church of Visitation and to the Twentieth Anniversary of the Saint Michael's Catholic Slovak Society in Winnipeg), Winnipeg, Man., 1957.

Richmond, Anthony H., *Post-War Immigrants in Canada*, Toronto, 1967.

Sadler, John Edward, *J. A. Comenius and the Concept of Universal Education*, London, 1966.

Saywell, J. T. (ed.), *Canadian Annual Review*, Annual vols. for chapter on immigration and immigration policy, Toronto.

Skelton, O. D., *The Railway Builders*, vol. XXXII of G. M. Wrong and H. H. Langton, (eds.), *The Chronicles of Canada*, Toronto, Glasgow, 1914–16.

Slavs in Canada, Inter-University Committee on Canadian Slavs, Edmonton, 1966.

Smith, W. G., *A Study in Canadian Immigration*, Toronto, 1920.

Timlin, M. F., "Economic Theory and Immigration Policy," *Canadian Journal of Economics and Political Science*, 16 (Aug. 1950).

—— "Canada's Immigration Policy," *ibid.*, 26 (Nov. 1960).

Tlapák, Václav, "Situace našich zemědělců v Kanadě" ("The Situation of Our Agricultural Workers in Canada"), *Naše Zahraničí*, Journal for the problems of emigration, 1 (Prague, 1931).

Watson, Omar K., "Moraviatown, 1869," Ontario Historical Society, *Papers and Records*, 28 (1932).

Wood, William, *The Fight for Canada*, 1904.

Czech and Slovak Canadian periodicals.

CHAPTER THREE

Organization of the ethnic group

One cannot appreciate the aims and consequent actions of immigrants to Canada, as individuals and as members of ethnic groups, unless one continually reminds oneself that this country has never been a melting pot of peoples; and that both personal inclination and official encouragement have led the newcomers to attempt integration into the Canadian community rather than assimilation by one of its two dominant components, the British or the French. Consequently, members of ethnic groups in Canada have stronger motives to stick together than those in other immigrants' havens such as the United States. This is not to say that, there, ethnic groups do not show coherence; they do, in many cases, and the American Czechs and Slovaks are a good example of this. The difference is that to promote cultural (and thereby a necessary degree of social) diversity is against the spirit of United States immigration; it is not at all against the spirit of Canadian.

For the earlier immigrants, naturally enough, material considerations were foremost. A newcomer to Canada was still largely left to his own devices; he had to think first of mere survival in a strange environment and next of gaining a firm economic footing. In those pioneer days—pioneer for the Czechs and Slovaks in Canada, at any rate—conditions forbade an immigrant from sitting back and taking a mental inventory, as it were. Cultural endeavours were then still the preserve of the native elements, who were financially better saddled and socially more prominent. Only gradually did the immigrants enter the higher, non-materialistic spheres of Canadian life.

The Czech and Slovak communities in Canada began to organize as soon as they were numerous enough to make it worthwhile. Even then, and for some time to come, they were handicapped by the lack of natural community leaders. Only gradually did such come to the fore and were fellowships formed. Their natural focal points were the church, the society for mutual economic assistance, the quasi-political national association, and the cultural centre of one kind or the other, such as the ethnic newspaper. They all played a role in the lives of the Czech and Slovak immigrants to Canada, and in the development of their communities. This role was apt to be most important, and sometimes decisive, for the first generation. And it often remains significant as well for the following, though fully integrated, generations.

THE CHURCH

About 80 per cent of the Czechs and Slovaks in Canada are Catholics, the great majority of the Roman, a much smaller number, of the Greek rite. The lack of Czech and Slovak priests during the first half century of Czech and Slovak immigration was less acutely felt by the Roman Catholics since the language of the mass was then still exclusively Latin. This made regular observance possible. That is why in the first church building, erected in 1905 by the Slovak miners in Coleman, Alberta, the faithful could be served by priests of various backgrounds—initially by a Dutch and a Flemish priest.

The first Slovak Roman Catholic parish—and the first Czech or Slovak congregation of any denomination in Canada—was founded in Fort William, Ontario, as early as 1907. It was that of Saints Peter and Paul near the coal docks of the big inland harbour where many Slovaks were employed as labourers. The pastor when its church was built, in 1911, was a remarkable man, a French Jesuit priest, Father Francis Maynard, who learned Slovak to be able to minister to the spiritual needs of his flock. The first Slovak priest for Saints Peter and

Paul's, Father Pazúrik, only arrived from the old country some time after the First World War. Then Fathers Hudák and Vodička administered the parish until 1934, when the Slovak Benedictines took it over for the next sixteen years. Since 1950 Father Joseph Reguly, a son of the community, has been the pastor. It is a big congregation, numbering at present some twelve hundred, and is particularly active in the educational and social spheres.

Fort William was an exception, however. Generally, Czech and Slovak Catholics depended on the occasional mission from the United States for instruction and advice in their mother tongue until well into the twenties and thirties of this century.

In Chatham, Ontario, for instance, where a strong ethnic group had settled soon after the First World War, regular missions were held by Father Tománek from 1928 onwards. They quickly led to the establishment of a parish association—without church and parish, though—named for Saints Cyril and Method, with the initial membership a respectable 130. It continued to be spiritually guided by periodic missions until the arrival, in 1941, of Father Frank Dostál. Ordained in Dublin, Ireland, the previous year, he was the first Czech Jesuit to be stationed permanently (as far as this can ever be said of a member of that order) in Canada. Before he could establish a Chatham parish, he was transferred to Batawa, Ontario, returning to Chatham only in 1948. The following year, the congregation which had existed—and had stuck together—for some twenty years got its church, St. Anthony's. The spirit of the old Association of Saints Cyril and Method carries on in Chatham, more recently under the direction of Father Mlýnský, CC.

Much the same thing happened in western Canada. Winnipeg even before the First World War had a strong enough Czech and Slovak community to allow the establishment of a parish in which the spiritual needs of the group would be ministered to in the mother tongue. Again, the obstacle was the lack of a pastor. There was hope of acquiring one when in 1922 a young Oblate priest of Slovak descent, Father George Šalamon, came to western Canada, but he was able to stay only for a short time. Thereafter, the best the faithful could expect were irregular missions, such as that of Father Florian Dobr

(Dobrovodský). Regular missions were conducted before 1939 by Slovak priests from the United States, Reverend Tondra and Reverend Oktavec, and after the outbreak of the war also by a Czech, Father Joseph Čelustka, CSsR. Otherwise, the Czechs and Slovaks joined local congregations, preferably those whose pastors spoke an intelligible Slavic language. Thus many Winnipeg Czechs and Slovaks worshipped in the Polish church of the Holy Ghost; and some, especially if they came from eastern Slovakia and thus were accustomed to hear Ruthenian spoken, joined Greek-rite Catholic, Ukrainian congregations. In the meantime, a parish association was formed, as in Chatham, at first without church or parish, the St. Michael Catholic Slovak Society. The opportunity to acquire a pastor arose in the fall of 1947 when the society got in touch with Reverend John Rekem, who had fled from Czechoslovakia into Austria from the persecutions that preceded the full-scale communist coup of February 1948. His name was presented to the Archbishop of Winnipeg, and he was invited to come. In 1949, he took charge of ministering to the spiritual needs of Slovak Roman Catholics in the Winnipeg diocese, working at first out of Immaculate Conception parish. Finally, in 1952, with the consecration of the new church of the Visitation of Our Lady, Father Rekem became pastor of an independent congregation. This was just thirty years after the Winnipeg flock had first thought that they had found their own shepherd.

Even in the biggest Czech and Slovak community in Canada, that of Toronto, Roman Catholic parishes were established only after long delays and with much difficulty. It was again mainly the old obstacle of lack of pastors. At first, as in Winnipeg, the Toronto Slovaks affiliated themselves with Polish church organizations. This was the most convenient solution, since Polish, though not nearly as easily understood by a Slovak as is Czech, is the Slavic language next most intelligible to him. Thus Slovak Catholic life for a while centred around the Polish church of St. Stanislaus and the Polish Hall. There, too, from 1927 onwards, were formed the First Catholic Slovak Alliance, and the Toronto branches of the (American) Slovak Catholic Sokol and the Pennsylvanian Slovak Catholic Club. They received spiritual guidance from Slovak priests who came to Toronto from the

United States, at first irregularly. A regular mission was established in
1932 by an American Slovak priest, Father Amand Kopáč. Finally, in
1934, a young chaplain from Ohio, Father Michael Shuba, was appointed, initially for two years and then permanently. In the following
year, the Slovak Catholic parish of Toronto, that of Saints Cyril and
Method, was established. During the war a church was built, and in
1950 a parish hall. Today, the congregation is stronger than ever.
Father Shuba still guides it after thirty-three years. He has given his
life to the performance of his humble pastoral task in Toronto.

A Toronto Czech Roman Catholic parish came into being even later.
Admittedly, the idea was abroad for a long time, but the immediate
impulse for its realization was only given in 1951 when Father Berná-
ček visited the city and was urged to stay. The parish of St. Wenceslas
was formed, and the collection of money for a church building
vigorously tackled. Although some very heartening examples were set
—a Czech workman, for instance, in the hospital after a disabling
accident donated all his savings—it proved to be slow going. In the
meantime, a new pastor, Father Gerard Janda, who had previously
served in Chicoutimi, Quebec, arrived. Soon after, an old disused
cinema was acquired as St. Wenceslas' first church building. A new
one was started in the early sixties, to be consecrated by James
Cardinal McGuigan at Christmas 1963. It is an ethnic church throughout, largely financed by the congregation, designed by a Czech-
Canadian architect, Frank Štalmach, and built by a Czech-Canadian
construction firm. Joseph Cardinal Beran, the last primate of Czechoslovakia—he was exiled from the country in 1965 after many years of
internment—dedicated the cross of the altar, a replica of the famous
one of Myslbek in Prague, on the occasion of his visit to Toronto in
the spring of 1966.

The parish of Batawa, Ontario, founded by Father Dostál, we have
already mentioned. It was originally meant to serve the substantial
group of Czech and Slovak employees of the world-wide Bata concern, who with their families had come over in 1939 from the home
establishment in Zlín, Czechoslovakia, to found a factory and factory
settlement in Canada. The site is on the Trent River, north of Trenton,
Ontario. There, with the help of the company, and the contributions

of the faithful, the parish of the Sacred Heart was established and a church built. When Father Dostál left for Chatham, Father Gáborik, CC, who had come from the order house in Jerusalem, took over. The church has been for years now a centre of spiritual and cultural life in the community. The composition of the latter has changed, though. Many of the originals have gone, and the influx of new Czechs and Slovaks has been slight in more recent years. They are in a minority now in the congregation. Thus, quite naturally, Father Gáborik's successor in Batawa is already an Irish-Canadian priest.

There are now in Canada a good many Czech and Slovak parishes, and the founding of most of them has followed the pattern described. In Hamilton, Ontario, to cite one more instance, it worked this way: establishment of a Catholic Circle in 1932, served spiritually by missionary visits from the Benedictine Order in Cleveland, Ohio; arrival of a permanent pastor, Father Füzy, in 1950; consecration of the parish church in 1953. Windsor, Ontario, has the second oldest regular Slovak congregation in Canada; it was established by Father Maty in 1927. The westernmost is in New Westminster, British Columbia. It, too, bears the name of St. Cyril and Method, and is currently administered by Father Lacko, SJ.

After the long years of dearth of shepherds for the Czech and Slovak Roman Catholic flocks in Canada, there is now a modest "reservoir." The Jesuit Order has a Czech House in Montreal, and a Slovak House in Galt, Ontario, with about five and eight resident members, respectively, at any one time. This comparatively strong foothold in Canada is surprising, considering the hard times the Society of Jesus had in the Czech and Slovak lands of Austria and later in Czechoslovakia itself. The Jesuits first came to Prague in 1556, and to Trnava, in Slovak Upper Hungary, in 1561. A Bohemian Province of the Order was established in 1623. But then the temporary suppression of the Society of Jesus by Pope Clement XIV in 1773 was followed by Emperor Joseph II's general ordinances against the religious houses only a few years later. The Jesuits were driven out of the Habsburg domains, and they took some time recovering their positions. Even so, before 1938 and Munich, the members of the Czechoslovak Province of Jesuits numbered 391. Then, two new waves of persecution, more cruel than those of the eighteenth century, engulfed the Order—the Nazi and the communist. After German concentration camps came Czechoslovak communist labour camps. Only a handful of Czech and Slovak Jesuits escaped to the free world.

The Slovak Jesuits settled in Canada some fifteen years earlier than their Czech brethren. Both are under the jurisdiction of the Order's Upper Canadian Province in Toronto. After the mission house of the Slovak Jesuits in Guelph, Ontario, burnt down, they moved to a new property in Galt, whence they have been carrying out their work under the direction of their superior, Father Žabka, SJ. Their mission activities are especially extensive in the many places in Canada where Slovak communities lack a priest of their language. Thus, in western Canada Father Dančo performs regular missionary work. Besides, they also give pastoral aid to the fifteen established Slovak Canadian Roman Catholic parishes. Father Senčík and Father Moravský are particularly active in the literary sphere.

The Czech mission house, in Montreal, was organized in 1960 when Father Feřt came to the city as the first superior. Built on land donated by Loyola College, the mission house of Saints Cyril and Method was consecrated by Paul Cardinal Léger in 1961. It also contains the Cultural Centre of Cardinal Beran. The present acting superior is Father Hořák, SJ. Among the residents is Father Lang, who lectures on the fine arts at Loyola College and is himself an outstanding painter and sculptor. His works can be seen in a number of places in Canada, for instance at the Jesuit seminary in Willowdale, Ontario, at St. Anthony's in Chatham, Ontario, and at the Church of the Redemptorists at Sherbrooke, Quebec.

The great majority of the Greek-rite Catholics came originally from the eastern parts of Slovakia. Quite naturally, they at first worshipped in Canada in the fairly numerous Ukrainian churches of their faith. It was only in 1936 that the head of the Greek Catholic Diocese of Canada, Bishop Ladyka, began to encourage the Slovak faithful to form their own congregations. These, as was the case with the Roman Catholic, had to depend initially on missions, conducted in this instance mainly by the orders of the Basilians and the Redemptorists. For years, Fathers Križanovský, Chanát, Rusňák, and in Montreal

The Honourable Paul Hellyer and Sokols at Masaryktown

Top: Gustav Přístu[

Bottom. Left: Masaryk Hall in Toronto. Right: Captain Jerry Kasan[

Opening ceremony of
a Sokol slet in Canada

Major Arthur Adams, of the Royal
Canadian Legion, and John A.
Mráček of Branch 601, Czechoslovak,
of the Legion

Bishop Michael Rusňák

Mrs. Ruth Petříček

Prokop Havlík

Stephen Rudinský

even a French priest, the Reverend Josaphat, a veritable latter-day Father Maynard of Fort William, did yeoman work. In due course, the first permanent parish organizations were established in Lethbridge, Alberta, and in Montreal. In the latter city, Bishop Izidor Borecký himself put things in motion for the formation of a Slovak Greek Catholic parish, with Father Havryluk as pastor. This was in 1949. In 1960, the cornerstone was laid for its new church—built, incidentally, by a Slovak Canadian, Andrew Midlík—the Slovak Catholic Church of the Ascension (Eastern Rite). In Lethbridge, the very active parish of Saints Peter and Paul maintains, apart from the church building proper, a social centre, the Slovak Hall, erected in 1958.

In the meantime, two Redemptorist Fathers, the Reverend Dr. Mina and the Reverend Michael Rusnák, went about establishing Greek Catholic parishes in Ontario. The former founded those in Toronto (1951), in Windsor, and in Sudbury; Reverend Rusnák those in Hamilton, Oshawa, and Welland. Of these, the Hamilton community has become particularly prominent. Its large hall, the Cultural Centre of Greek Catholic Slovaks in Canada, inaugurated just before Christmas 1957, aims to serve "all Greek Catholic Slovaks in North America and be a symbolic centre in the Free World." The Slovak Greek Catholic church magazine, the monthly *Maria*, first published in Windsor in 1954, was also later moved to Hamilton.

In October 1964 came formal recognition from the Holy See of the importance of the work done. Reverend Rusnák, CSsR, was appointed Apostolic Visitator of the Slovak Catholics of Byzantine rite in Canada and Auxiliary Bishop to Bishop Borecký. His diocese is Cernik, in today's Albania and thus indeed *in partibus infidelium*. At the same time, it has its significance in terms of Czech and Slovak history, for it is closely connected with the bishopric of Ochrid, which St. Clement, the great disciple of Saints Cyril and Method, headed in the ninth century. Bishop Rusnák's official seat is in Toronto.

The Czech and Slovak Baptists in Canada have a special link with this country's past through the Moravian Brethren who, as we showed in a previous chapter, played a role in early Canadian history. The Baptist families who came to Canada from (then) Polish Volhynia and settled around Minitonas, Manitoba, were the direct descendants of those Brethren whom Comenius had led into exile after the Battle of the White Mountain, three centuries before. Some of them later moved to Toronto, to swell a Baptist congregation, many of whose members also trace their ancestry back to the originals of the Unitas Fratrum.

Baptist religious work among the Czech and Slovak Canadians was first undertaken in Windsor, Ontario, and has continued since. The moving spirits were two families—one Slovak, the Gažos, and one Czech, the Valentas. In the beginning, Windsor was merely a missionary station of the Detroit church, visited by the Reverend Čatloš of Chicago. It became independent in 1927, with a permanent pastor, the Reverend John Fořt. In 1955, the Reverend Zajíček, the veteran Czech-Canadian Baptist preacher, came to Windsor after years of highly successful missionary work in western Canada and an outstanding pastorate of the new Toronto Baptist congregation. Under his leadership, the new church in Windsor was built in 1960. Reverend Zajíček also serves the Czech and Slovak faithful in neighbouring towns, Chatham, Harrow, Blenheim, and Leamington.

The Minitonas Baptists first organized themselves into a congregation in 1929, under an active lay preacher, Wenceslas Moravec. By 1932, a church building had been dedicated by the growing community under its pastor, Reverend V. Vojta. It supports, among other good causes, the monthly church magazine, *The Vinyard*, edited by Frank Hlubuček. Another very active Czech and Slovak Baptist congregation is in Glenside, Saskatchewan. There, the beginnings of church work may even go back to 1910, when there seems to have been a meeting place in Glenside, the Hus Chapel.

In Winnipeg, it was the acknowledged leader of the Czech community, Frank Dojáček, who was also instrumental in initiating Baptist religious work. In 1930, he laid the cornerstone to a mission which originally was called the Union of Chelčický and later became the Bethlehem Chapel of the Czechoslovak Baptist Church. These names again show the close and highly cherished connection of the Czech and Slovak Baptists in Canada with the early Protestantism of the Hussite period. In 1930 also, the Manitoba Baptist Convention ordained a Czech Canadian preacher, Reverend Charles Bohatec.

The Bethlehem Chapel became the focal point of missionary work across the prairies. Everywhere, in Rosewood, Dominion City, Morden, and other places, it has supported the Baptist laymen who organized the local church groups. From Winnipeg came the first impulse for the formation of a Baptist community even in Toronto.

Here again, the name crops up of the indefatigable Frank Dojáček, who provided the moral spur and by his assurance of initial financial assistance removed the first material obstacles. Work started in 1942 under the leadership of two lay preachers, the Czech Charles Jelínek and the Slovak George Fabok. Two years later, the Reverend Zajíček arrived as the congregation's first ordained preacher. From then on, the community has grown steadily. Since late 1960, and under the present pastor, Reverend Joseph Novák, its services in Czech and Slovak at the big Parkdale Baptist church are now well attended by members of other denominations who want to hear the singing and sermons in the mother tongue. The choirs, incidentally, have gained a deservedly wide reputation. Phonograph records have been made of their renderings of old Czech and Slovak church songs.

The Czech and Slovak Baptists in Canada, both the established church communities and the many smaller groups led by lay preachers, are united in the Czechoslovak Baptist Convention of the United States and Canada. Through it, and through the Canadian Baptist Federation and the Baptist World Alliance, they support missionary work in many places abroad. Up to 1948, when the communist coup closed the door, they worked in this way in Czechoslovakia also.

The Slovak Lutherans, too, began to form church communities soon after the First World War. In Toronto, missionary services had started by 1922. A parish could, however, be established only in 1942, under the presidency of Michael Bartolomej and with the Reverend John Horárik as pastor. At first called John the Baptist Lutheran, it is now St. Paul's. A new church building was acquired in 1959. Subsequently the Reverend P. Jamnický served the congregation; their present pastor is the Reverend D. Jurkovič who preaches in Slovak as well as in English. It is significant that the founding families are still in the forefront of church work. The congregation also takes a particularly active part in the cultural and social life of the Czech and Slovak community in Toronto.

The Reverend John Horárik, who was present at the foundation of the Toronto Lutheran parish, came to Canada in 1928, having been sent by the Missouri Synod of the Lutheran Church to Montreal to attend to the spiritual needs of the faithful there. The budding congregation went through difficult times during the Great Depression. It met wherever hospitality was offered, the German Lutheran church, the Presbyterian, the French Baptist. It was not until 1938 that a parish—of the Church of the Ascension—was formally established. Arrangements were still rather makeshift, though church work was attended to regularly. Finally, in 1952, under the pastorate of the Reverend Emil Velebir, the congregation was able to build a church which it now shares with the English-speaking Lutherans of Montreal.

There are now a number of Slovak Lutheran parishes, especially in Ontario: Christ Evangelical Lutheran Church in Timmins, the achievement of the Slovak miners of the region, with a church building erected in 1950; the Church of Our Saviour in Chatham, which has a membership drawn from a number of ethnic groups; Holy Trinity in Bradford, serving the Slovak farmers and market gardeners of Holland Marsh; churches at Smithville, Barrie, Aurora. Everywhere, the traditions are upheld of old-country Lutheranism, traditions of humanism and Czech and Slovak unity which influenced so significantly Slovak history.

Finally, there are Slovak Pentecostal Assemblies in Toronto, Oshawa, and Leamington, Ontario, the last-named being the largest. Reverends Fred Tinus, of Cooksville, and Andrew Sich, of Leamington, lead the faithful.

The history of Czech and Slovak religious life in Canada is important also because it is so characteristic of the whole development of the ethnic groups. The desire to stand together is always present, as is the desire to hear the word of God in the mother tongue. This desire persists also in later generations—in the Baptist congregations, in particular, where only a very few members have been born in Czechoslovakia or have as much as seen the old country—even when the habitual language is already English. The formation of parishes is always difficult. The early parishioners are invariably humble folk, manual workers with more faith and enthusiasm than organizational ability and money. But the obstacles are cleared away, little by little.

The widow's mite provides the down-payment for the church. The penniless immigrant of the post-1919 years becomes well established. The old guard is swelled by an influx of better educated co-nationals. In the end, the building is done, in the literal as well as in the derived sense. The church stands, with a congregation which has remained closely knit through all the years of adversity, as one of the foci of the life of the ethnic group.

THE SOCIETY FOR

MUTUAL ECONOMIC ASSISTANCE

Canada has always been a good country for immigration, but at one time it was a hard one for the unlucky or unsuccessful. The foundations of the comprehensive system of social security which we have today were only laid during the Second World War, its principal pillar, federal unemployment insurance, being enacted in 1941. This was decades after the protection of the socially weak had become commonplace in many countries of Europe. If it was perhaps believed that such protection would be unnecessary in a country of seemingly limitless opportunities, the Great Depression brought a rude awakening. Remedial action, though reasonably prompt, came too late to save many people from grave hardships. These fell in particular upon the immigrants whose economic base was as a rule even less secure than that of the average native Canadian.

The need for self-help through mutual assistance was thus a pressing one in Canada in the first four decades of this century. Consequently, the first Czech and Slovak fraternal organizations of any consequence in this country were of the mutual benefit kind. They sprang from a desire for self-preservation in a country where there was no public sickness and death insurance as yet, and private insurance as a rule was too expensive for the little man. Only gradually did the benevolent societies move also into the social and cultural fields. The initiative usually came from the members for whom the society was a kind of general centre of group activity. This in the end brought in some political undertones also—and, as we will see, more than that in some cases. With that, the mutual benefit association became the focal point of just about everything that was going on among its membership, from economic pursuits to politics, from recreation to publishing in the native language.

As far as the Czechs and Slovaks were concerned, the first step toward satisfying these needs was taken in Winnipeg. Again it was Frank Dojáček who was the moving spirit. On April 27, 1913, seventy persons, mostly Czechs but some also from other Slavic nationalities, met and fifty-four of them took the plunge and became founding members of the Czecho-Slav Benevolent Association of Winnipeg. It was a voluntary organization not under a formal insurance charter, whose purposes, as they were laid down from the beginning, were to bring together citizens of Slavic origin, assist them in cases of illness and death in the family, support ethnic activities, especially educational, and keep alive the knowledge and use of the mother tongue.

Right from the start, this Association was a huge success. Especially during the First World War it became the one firm centre in Canada for Czech and Slovak patriotic action. In co-operation with the older and much more powerful national organizations in the United States, it gave encouragement and material support to the Czechoslovak National Council in Paris. It propagated the idea, entirely new to Canadians, of an independent Czechoslovak state. And it gave a helping hand in the formation of the Bohemian Detachment of the 223rd Battalion of the Canadian Expeditionary Force. From among the early workers in the Association, apart from Frank Dojáček and his brother Joseph, the names Dvořák, Pátek, Ruda, Štětina, are still gratefully remembered by present-day members.

After the founding of the new Czechoslovakia, the name of the society was changed to Czechoslovak Benevolent Association. Immediately after the war, in 1919, and entirely from members' contributions, it acquired a home of its own, on Winnipeg's McKenzie Street, in which it is still located. From there, the Association conducted its activities, which in the first thirty years were primarily economic, and also its work in the social and cultural fields. A good Czech, Slovak, and English library was assembled. A ladies' auxiliary and youth groups were formed. Sports events were sponsored. Supplementary school classes in the mother tongue, as well as English courses for newcomers, were organized. The Association's head-quarters is now called the Czechoslovak National House, and this it is in the truest sense of the word. It was there that the fiftieth anniversary of the foundation of the old Czecho-Slav Benevolent Association was celebrated in 1963. One of the authors of this book, who attended the festive occasion, was amazed to see how strong the pride was in their Czech or Slovak origin among some of the children who represented the fourth generation of families who had come to the west before the First World War.

The next attempt to organize an economic-social-cultural co-operative for the Czechs and Slovaks was less successful. In 1924, there was formed in Montreal the Czechoslovak Mutual Benefit Society. It made an energetic drive for members and at first attracted a fair number of them, especially among the Slovak labourers of the region. A branch office was opened in Toronto in 1927, and for some years before the war played an important role in the national community. Later on, however, whether for good reason or not, public confidence was lost, and the Czechoslovak Mutual Benefit Society disappeared from the scene.

A new initiative was taken, again in western Canada, when in 1928 the First Slovak Mutual Benefit Society was founded in Blairmore, Alberta. This, the first of the coal-mining towns of the Crow's Nest Pass region, had had a fair-sized Slovak community even before the First World War, and also an enthusiastic—one might say a visionary—community leader in George Kleskeň, a printer and, despite many disappointments, an undaunted newspaper publisher. The Society was a common project of men from a number of surrounding places, Hillcrest, Bellevue, Coleman, Natal, Fernie. The idea caught on, and local branches sprang up in Lethbridge, Alberta; New Westminster, British Columbia; Regina and Estevan, Saskatchewan. Commonly known as the "Western Society," it published for a time its own news-papers, first *Úvahy* ("Deliberations"), and then *Hlas Národa* (Voice of the Nation"). In this, the initiator was, of course, Kleskeň. Otherwise, the chief officials of the Society were John Dančo and Louis Kalivoda. Although then a very young organization, it proved itself in the Great Depression when it helped many of its members to help themselves through the bad times.

The eastern Canadian equivalent of the Western Society came into being in Kirkland Lake, Ontario, in the summer of 1932. Its official title was The National Slovak Mutual Benefit Society of Canada, but, naturally enough, it was generally referred to as the "Eastern Society." One of its founders, and long-time driving spirit and president, was Edward Oravec. It went farther than its predecessors in that it secured a regular insurance charter in 1934. At first active mainly in the mining towns of Kirkland Lake, Timmins, Noranda, and Sudbury, it eventually went farther afield, establishing branches in such big centres as Toronto, Montreal, Windsor, and Sarnia. The Eastern Society was an efficiently run organization which concentrated on its primary job of providing sickness and death benefits to its members, without, however, neglecting the usual social and cultural activities of fraternal organizations of this kind.

The Canadian Slovak League is an offshoot of the American organization of that name formed in Cleveland, Ohio, in 1907, but for the last thirty-five years it has been entirely independent. It was as a local branch of the latter that it was established in Winnipeg in 1926. It provided the nucleus for the Canadian Slovak League, formally founded at a congress in that city in December 1932. The moving spirits were George Rondoš, who has been called the "father of the Slovak immigrants" because of his life-long devoted work on their behalf, Julius and Anne Rezník, Andrew Matuský, and Andrew Kučera, the league's first chairman and still its grand old man. Kučera was a recipient of the Coronation Medal of 1953. Branches were thereafter established in quick succession all over Canada, up to a peak number of sixty-three. At present, there are fifty-four branches and twenty-six youth groups, with a total membership in excess of 3,200. The Canadian Slovak League is thus the biggest purely Slovak association in this country.

From 1934 onwards, the Canadian Slovak League has operated as a mutual benefit society, albeit for the first twenty years on a voluntary basis. A federal insurance charter was obtained in October 1954. A congress at Fort William, Ontario, at the end of that same month, carried out the resultant corporate changes in the organization. Still, although the economic activities of the League have been extensive and its financial resources now exceed all of 1.1 million dollars, its main importance remains in the social, cultural, and political, fields.

The Canadian Slovak League has always stressed its "Christian, democratic, nationalist, and decidedly anti-communist" character. In practice, the terms "Christian" and "nationalist" have been interpreted restrictively; although those belonging to other denominations are not debarred from membership, the League is a Catholic organization, and it favours an independent Slovakia. Like its American counterpart, it has departed a long way from the original policies of the League, which in the First World War contributed much to the eventual establishment of a free Czechoslovakia. Very generally speaking, the cleavage in the Slovak community is between those who want to see the Slovaks go it alone, and thus join the League if they join any organization of the ethnic group, and those who favour the fraternal link with the Czechs, and would consequently be found in the ranks of the Czechoslovak National Association. Within the boundaries set by its philosophy, the Canadian Slovak League pursues its stated aims of assisting its members to become good citizens— in other words, to integrate with the Canadian community, and uplifting them economically, socially, morally, and culturally.

As far as organization is concerned, the central office of the League holds the association capital needed for the fulfilment of its social insurance function, and publishes its paper, *Kanadský Slovák* ("Canadian Slovak"), as well as the yearly *Almanack* of the Canadian Slovak League. The branches own their own properties, the most important of which are the National Halls, like those in Winnipeg, Toronto, Montreal, St. Catharines, and Welland, Ontario. The one in Montreal is the most remarkable, and realizes a dream which may once have seemed over-ambitious for an ethnic group of modest size and means. Called the Canadian-Slovak Cultural Centre, it was erected between the summer of 1957 and the fall of 1958 by a Slovak-Canadian builder, Steve Sura, at a cost of one-and-a-half million dollars. As its name indicates, its main purpose is to provide a focal point for educational, artistic, and other cultural activities.

In 1934, after taking on a mutual benefit function, the Slovak Benefit Society of Canada was founded and became a member of the Independent Mutual Benefit Federation with headquarters in Toronto. The Society has always been suspected of being a radically leftist organization. There is evidence that this was indeed its official leaning, and to a degree probably still is. Thus, in 1940, its newspaper, the *Hlas ľudu* ("Voice of the People"), was suppressed by the authorities together with other communist (or at any rate, fellow-travelling) periodicals which, after the Russo-German pact of August 1939, and before Germany's attack on its Soviet ally in June 1941, opposed the war as imperialist. After 1941, the Society, of course, supported the war effort and also the movement for the liberation of Czechoslovakia, Many of its officials and members thus took an active part in the work of the Czechoslovak National Alliance (see below). Its present position can be deduced from the statement that the Society's "membership in general has a positive attitude to present-day Czechoslovakia."

Whatever the Slovak Benefit Society of Canada's political slant may be, it certainly remains very active in the social and cultural life of the community. With about a thousand full members and several branches throughout Canada, it maintains halls in Toronto and Fort William, and contributes to the maintenance of the Czechoslovak People's Hall in Windsor. It runs recreation camps at Streetsville near Toronto, Joliette near Montreal, and outside Windsor. Its folklore groups, like the Tatra Dancers of Toronto or the Dolina Ensemble of Montreal, have given public performances in a number of places, including Expo '67. The Society also has some Czech members. Its long-time president is John Džatko, and its equally long-time secretary Michael Kijovský. The official organ since 1941 is called *L'udové zvesti* ("People's News"), and is edited by Joseph Ďurjančik, also a Society old-timer, who has worked for it and its predecessor since 1933.

We now have to come back to the two original Slovak mutual benefit associations, the older Western Society and the younger Eastern Society. The two joined their operations after a common meeting in Sudbury, Ontario, in 1946. Six years later, they also gave themselves one name, that of Canadian Slovak Benefit Society, admittedly not too well chosen because of its similarity to that of the Slovak Benefit Society of Canada. With a federal insurance charter and some forty-five branches, it operates from coast to coast. Like the other fraternal organizations, the Canadian Slovak Benefit Society also maintains National Halls, like those in Sarnia, Sudbury, New Westminster, and Beverly just outside Edmonton. It also has a big recreation centre in Vaughan township, not far from Toronto, named "Štefániktown" after the Slovak member of the triumvirate who led the fight for Czechoslovak independence in the First World War. Instrumental in the development of this united society have been their subsequent presidents, J. Lipovský, Paul Šemetka, Paul Chvostek, and George Baláž as well as the old-time treasurer M. Mart'an. Although the Society has no official political affiliation, its membership of about 3,000 generally supports Czech and Slovak unity.

The social and cultural activities of the Society are extensive. They are aimed both at the better integration of the membership in the Canadian community and at the preservation of the group's cultural heritage. Thus, help is being given to members wishing to improve their general education, and instruction and encouragement is given especially to the young, to preserve their knowledge of the homeland. In pursuit of this double goal, the Society also publishes a newspaper, *Slovenský Hlas* ("Slovak Voice"), which first came out in Windsor in 1949, but was transferred to Toronto two years later. The "Slovak Voice"'s first editor was L. Gorek; its second, from 1951 to 1955, was Michael Ferik, at present an Ontario economist; and now, for over a decade, its devoted editor has been Andrew Kováč, better known to the ethnic community by his pen-name, O. M. Debnárkin.

Quite a number of American fraternal societies also have Canadian members, for instance the First Catholic Slovak Union, the Slovak Evangelical Union, the Slovak National Society.

Of a somewhat different kind from the old benevolent societies are the financial co-operatives founded after the Second World War, when Canadians already enjoyed the benefits of a comprehensive system of social security and there was no need for private citizens to provide mutual economic protection. The idea behind these new institutions is to give the best individual service at the lowest overhead cost, such as is possible only in a smaller group closely knit by common background and interest. A typical co-operative is the thriving Czechoslovak (Toronto) Credit Union Limited, which after only fifteen years of existence has close to a thousand members, and assets comparable to those of older and more far-flung benefit societies. Characteristically it calls itself "Kampelička," after one of the two types of saving co-operatives common in pre-war rural Czechoslovakia. Unlike the Canadian Slovak League or the Slovak Benefit Society, the Czechoslovak Credit Union is primarily a financial institution not a society with mixed economic, social, cultural, or even political purposes.

THE QUASI-POLITICAL

NATIONAL ASSOCIATION

There is in the Czech and Slovak community the kind of frankly and exclusively political club with aims related entirely to the European homeland. The Slovaks have one composed of post-1945 refugees who continue to carry the message of the short-lived Slovak State (1939–45), despite the handicap that it was a military ally of Germany and Italy and at war with Canada. There were in fact originally two such groups in Canada, the Slovak National Council Abroad and the Slovak Liberation Committee, but they merged in 1960 in a single Slovak Liberation Council. The opposite point of view is represented by the Canadian section of the Council of Free Czechoslovakia. Its chairman, significantly, has for many years been a Slovak Canadian, Rudolph Fraštacký.

In a way, the Czechoslovak National Association in Canada continues to function as a liberation movement, with the immediate aim of keeping alive the idea of a free, democratic Czechoslovakia as the common homeland of the Czechs and Slovaks and as a state based on the humanist principles of its greatest founding father, Thomas Garrigue Masaryk. The association is, however, also a mass organization with many tasks, most of them related to Czech and Slovak life in Canada. It, too, is one of those multi-purpose ethnic organizations of which we have spoken earlier. If we have put it under the heading of "quasi-political association," it is because its original concerns have always remained relevant to its work.

The Czechoslovak National Association came into being because there was a need for a strong central organization of the Czech and Slovak Canadians to help in the war effort and thereby contribute to the liberation of Czechoslovakia. Such a need was already felt in the First World War. At that time, however, the national group was too weak numerically and too scattered to do much about it. Still, a branch was formed in Winnipeg of the Czechoslovak National Association in the United States, which had its headquarters in Chicago. Through this branch, Czech and Slovak Canadians were able to join the Czechoslovak National Council in America, which also comprised the (US—the Canadian did not exist yet) Slovak League and the National Alliance of Czech Catholics and which contributed much to the ultimate success of the struggle for an independent Czechoslovakia.

Between the wars there were various attempts to build a roof organization for the many societies and clubs that had formed within the two ethnic groups. Nothing came of it, precisely because a single, powerful objective was missing that would override divergent, often purely local, interests. Such a unifying goal was only found when Czechoslovakia lost her independence again in March 1939. Compared to that tragedy, everything else then became secondary. Under the leadership of a Slovak Canadian, Stephen Rudinský of Montreal, and a Czech Canadian, Gustav Přístupa of Toronto, the obstacles to unity were swept away. A joint committee of the national organizations was formed and met in Toronto on May 7, 1939. The establishment of a National Alliance of Slovaks, Czechs, and Subcarpathian Ruthenians in Canada was quickly decided upon. By June 24 and 25 of that year its first congress was held in Toronto's Church of All Nations. It was attended by 140 delegates and elected an executive, which eventually served all through the war, with Stephen Rudinský as chairman and Charles Buzek, a Czech Canadian from Toronto, as secretary-general. The cumbersome name of the association was soon changed to the simpler Czechoslovak National Alliance in Canada.

Practically all the Czech and Slovak organizations that were active at the time co-operated in the Czechoslovak National Alliance, with the sole and notable exception of the Canadian Slovak League. After the constitution of the Slovak State in March 1939, and its adherence to the Axis, the League found itself in a difficult position. Many among its leaders sympathized with the authoritarian regime of Dr. Tiso and his Hlinka's Slovak People's party, yet even if they had wished to support it actively—and few probably ever wanted to go that far—this would have been committing treason under Canadian law. So, the League decided to aid the Canadian war effort by collecting money for the Red Cross and similar activities, but to do it separately from the rest of the Czech and Slovak community united in the Czechoslovak National Alliance.

Carried forward by its own drive and by the general enthusiasm for the war against Nazi Germany, the alliance grew rapidly, from forty-six local branches in 1939 to a peak of eighty-six branches with some 6,500 members by the end of 1942. Two coast-to-coast organizational trips helped in this encouraging development. The first, financed by the alliance itself, was undertaken by Charles Buzek and a leading Slovak member of the organization, Peter Klimko. The Canadian Clubs made possible the other, by Senator Vojta Beneš, elder brother of the second president of Czechoslovakia, Dr. Edward Beneš, and two officers of the Czechoslovak forces abroad, Colonel John Ambruš and Captain Rudolph Nekola. The last-named, incidentally, eventually returned to this country after the communist coup of 1948, and became a Canadian citizen and editor of the weekly *Nový Domov* ("New Homeland"). The alliance administered the Czechoslovak War Charities Fund in Canada and collected about $331,000 for various causes connected with the war and the drive for the liberation of Czechoslovakia; and through its earnest endeavours, which gained it the respect of the Canadian authorities, helped bring about the decision, taken by Order in Council of April 10, 1941, recognizing Czechoslovak nationals in Canada as citizens of an allied country and thus not subject to wartime restrictions imposed on non-privileged aliens. This may not seem a great achievement today but it was a very important one at the time. After all, the exception granted applied to persons who, technically, were citizens either of the Protectorate of Bohemia-Moravia, which was a kind of German colony, or of the Slovak State, which was a German ally.

In the accompanying list are given the locations of the eighty-six wartime branches of the Czechoslovak National Alliance. We have included them not only in commemoration of a fine co-operative effort, unequalled since by the Czech and Slovak community in this country, but also as proof of the expansion of Czechs and Slovaks throughout the length and breadth of Canada in a mere sixty years. Among the place names, we still find the familiar ones of the early days, Esterhazy and Glenside, Saskatchewan; Minitonas, Manitoba; Frank, Blairmore, Coleman, Prague, Alberta. Of the original settlements, only Fernie, of bitter memories, is missing.

Branch number	Location	Branch number	Location
1	Kirkland Lake, Ont.	30	New Toronto, Ont.
2	Sarnia, Ont.	31	Fort William, Ont.
3	Niagara Falls, Ont.	33	Frank, Alta.
4	London, Ont.	34	Hamilton, Ont.
5	Port Colborne, Ont.	35	Evergreen, Alta.
6	Windsor, Ont.	36	Noranda, Que.
7	Chatham, Ont.	37	Arvida, Que.
8	Welland, Ont.	38	Blairmore, Alta.
9	Calgary, Alta.	39	Tilley, Alta.
10	Timmins, Ont.	41	Shaughnessy, Alta.
11	Duparquet, Que.	42	Coleman, Alta.
12	Oshawa, Ont.	43	Nacmine, Alta.
13	Temiscaming, Que.	44	Rosedale, Alta.
14	Iron Springs, Alta.	45	Bellevue, Alta.
16	West Toronto, Ont.	46	Viking-Prague, Alta.
17	Kenora, Ont.	47	Nordegg, Alta.
18	Vancouver, B.C.	48	Gerald, Sask.
19	Alvinston, Ont.	49	Sudbury, Ont.
20	Regina, Sask.	50	New Waterford, N.S.
21	Edmonton, Alta.	51	Montreal, Que.
22	Lethbridge, Alta.	52	Winnipeg, Man.
23	Nampa, Alta.	53	Steinbach, Man.
24	Toronto, Ont.	54	Tupper Creek, B.C.
25	Kitchener, Ont.	55	Glenside, Sask.
26	Michel, B.C.	56	Enderby, B.C.
27	Valley Centre, Sask.	57	New Westminster, B.C.
28	Val d'Or, Que.	58	Ladysmith, B.C.
29	Margo, Sask.	59	Flin Flon, Man.

Branch number	Location	Branch number	Location
60	Batawa, Ont.	75	St. Walburg, Sask.
61	Esterhazy, Sask.	76	Loon River, Sask.
62	Cranford, Alta.	77	Dominion City, Man.
63	Orono, Ont.	78	Minitonas, Man.
64	Saskatoon, Sask.	80	Henribourg, Sask.
65	Ruthven, Ont.	82	Port Arthur, Ont.
66	Prescott, Ont.	83	Morden, Sask.
67	Toronto 2, Ont.	84	Goodsoil, Sask.
68	St. Ann's, Ont.	85	North Battleford, Sask.
69	Springhill, N.S.	86	Galt, Ont.
70	St. Catharines, Ont.	87	Kingston, Ont.
71	Bradlo, Ont.	88	Delhi, Ont.
72	Woodstock, Ont.	89	Ottawa, Ont.
73	Nanaimo, B.C.	90	Canmore, Alta.
74	Fort Erie, Ont.	91	Victoria, B.C.

All through the war, the Czechoslovak National Alliance worked with signal success in many fields. Understandably, then, its Congress of Victory, held in November 1945 in Toronto, was a triumphant occasion. Under the chairmanship of John Gažo, a Slovak Canadian from Windsor, Ontario, the organization's wartime achievements were reviewed and tasks set for the peaceful future. Three principles were listed: first and foremost the promotion of good Canadian citizenship; the perpetuation of the Czech and Slovak cultural heritage; and material help to the old homeland which had just emerged from the destruction and privations of war and foreign occupation. The last of these three aims was furthered when the secretary-general of the Alliance, Charles Buzek, also became the executive director of the Canadian United Allied Relief Fund, a recognition of the extraordinarily successful work of the organization during the war.

With the war over, the centre of gravity in the Alliance shifted from the political to the social tasks, from interests abroad to interests at home. Thus, the Alliance submitted, in 1946 and 1947, two voluminous briefs to the Senate Standing Committee on Immigration and Labour, advocating certain legislative changes, a number of which were enacted in subsequent years. During this period right after the war action was initiated within the Alliance which aimed at providing a representative home for the Czech and Slovak community and which resulted in the building of Masaryk Hall and "Masaryktown."

The shift in emphasis in Alliance work—it was no more than that, for the interest in the "old country" remained very much alive—brought on its most serious crisis. When the communist "coup" occurred in Prague in late February 1948, the Alliance responded immediately with a strong declaration against that usurpation of power and, on the practical side, with the sponsoring of a relief organization, the Canadian Fund for Czechoslovak Refugees Incorporated. This, however, did not seem to be enough to many of the actual refugees from communism who came to Canada immediately after the coup, when escape from Czechoslovakia was considerably easier than later on. These men and women were bitterly disappointed and angry at seeing themselves exiles once more after less than three years of relatively free life in their homeland. Accordingly, they looked upon the Czech and Slovak national institutions in Canada, especially the big central organization, as bases from which to wage yet another struggle, the third in this century, for Czechoslovak liberation. To the old-timers, including all those who had been in Canada during the war, this was only one of several tasks, the urgency of which was a matter of priorities. The result was a cleavage between newcomers and old-timers. It seriously hindered the work of the Alliance for at least eight years, from 1948 to 1956.

The renewed upswing in the fortunes of the organization was due no doubt to new personalities and new policies, but in part also to external factors. One of these was the Hungarian revolt of 1956, which showed that liberation was not around the corner, and that much patience was needed. It became obvious, even to the most sanguine among the newcomers, that in the meantime the Alliance might well trim its sails and concentrate on less ambitious but also very important tasks, mainly domestic, social, and cultural. It was a return to and an elaboration of the far-sighted program already set out by the Victory Congress of 1945, and under its chairman, Frank Němec, who had once been the ambassador to Canada of free Czechoslovakia, the Alliance settled down again in 1956 to quiet, steady, and useful work.

Two other events of some import occurred at that time. The Alliance received a federal charter, which was presented to its

Eighteenth Congress in Hamilton, Ontario, in the fall of 1960, by the Minister of Citizenship and Immigration, Ellen Fairclough; and the name was changed to the present one of Czechoslovak National Association in Canada. With the return of inner stability, the Association has again grown and has extended its activities both at the central office and in the branches. Anthony Daičar, of Batawa, Ontario, who has served the organization in one capacity or another almost from its beginnings, is now central chairman, and George Corn, of Toronto, secretary-general. There are at present sixteen active branches and affiliated societies, as well as a good number of members-at-large. Even though its direct fee-paying membership after the above-mentioned cleavage is only about one-fifth of what it was in wartime, when one considers indirect members who participate in more specific cultural activities through the affiliated societies, the Czechoslovak National Association is a large organization again, in numbers and in performance, having survived its crisis and growing again in every respect. As its centennial project, the Association has taken the initiative toward the establishment of a chair of Czech and Slovak literature at the University of Toronto.

THE CULTURAL CENTRE

It would be impossible to enumerate, let alone describe, the activities of all the societies and clubs which have ever been formed within the Czech and Slovak community in Canada. To try to do so would in any case not serve the purpose of this book. Consequently, we have throughout dealt only with those institutions which continue to have a wider than local significance, those which have influenced the development of the national group. This criterion must be applied the more stringently in this section, which deals with activities in which the proliferation of associations is especially great. It should also be recalled that some of the organizations described in earlier sections of this chapter act not only in their primary functions, but also as focal points of social and cultural activities.

An institution which has had a formative, indeed at times a decisive, influence on the Czechs and Slovaks in their homeland, and is still important to them abroad, is the Sokol. The name means "falcon," evoking the picture of a noble bird, high-soaring, graceful, strong. Founded in 1862 by a professor of aesthetics and history of art at Charles University in Prague, Dr. Miroslav Tyrš, whose dream was the revival of the classical ideal of *kalokagathia* ("beauty and goodness"), in the Czech nation, the Sokol became a national institution. Although basically it was a gymnastic organization, it had the higher aim of moral regeneration of a long-oppressed people. From the beginning, the cream of the nation belonged to it: aristocrats like Prince Thurn-Taxis and Count Deym; the greatest of Czech historians, Francis Palacký; the writers F. L. Čelakovský and Karolina Světlá; the famous scientist John Purkyně; and politicians, journalists, artists, teachers; and it did not exclude the humble folk. The outstanding Czech painter Joseph Mánes designed the Sokol uniforms and emblems. In 1884 the Austrian government finally gave official sanction to the organization which had been listed in the police files as "a school of democracy, republicanism, and socialism," all heinous crimes in the old monarchy. At that time there were already eleven regional Sokol districts and 152 local units, with over 18,000 members. In the end, just before the Czechoslovak Sokol Organization was suppressed by the communist regime after 1948, the number of districts had grown to 52, of units to 3,367, and the membership to well over a million.

In Czechoslovakia, to be a patriot and to be a Sokol were almost synonymous. The president of the Republic was a member, and so was the boy or girl in elementary school. The Sokol *slets*—literally, "fly-togethers"—with their spectacular displays of mass calisthenics, were the supreme manifestations of the national spirit. The eleventh and last display in 1948, after the communist coup, was an impressive and deeply moving gesture of defiance which put new heart into sorely tried people, and made the official suppression of the Sokol inevitable. In sum, every good national cause in Czechoslovakia was the concern of the Sokol.

The Sokol idea also spread very soon into other countries. To serve the units in foreign lands, the special District of Sokols Abroad was formed in the Czech Sokol Organization, which after 1918 became the

Czechoslovak Sokol Organization. On this continent, the first Sokol unit was formed in St. Louis, Missouri, as early as 1865. Even in Canada, where, as we have seen, Czech and Slovak settlement began much later than in the United States and developed rather slowly, the first report of a unit's being established at Frank, Alberta, dates back to 1912. Before the First World War there were two more: a second one in the Crow's Nest Pass area, in Michel and Natal, British Columbia, and one at Goldburg, Saskatchewan. These were small groups which, especially in the mining region around Crow's Nest Pass with its fluctuating Czech and Slovak population, had a difficult time surviving. The Sokol organization in Canada took more definite form only after 1929 when it managed to put down roots in larger cities, Regina, Winnipeg, and Montreal. The Winnipeg unit was given the name of "Sokol Štefánik," and its first chairman, or "starosta," could, of course, have been no other than the indefatigable Frank Dojáček. The secretary was Louis Hnilo. The unit's present chairman, Joseph Hamata, incidentally, is also one of its founding members. "Sokol Masaryk" in Montreal, also founded in 1929, was followed three years later by a unit in Toronto, the first in Ontario. The next was in Batawa, Ontario, formed in 1941.

After the suppression of the Sokol in Czechoslovakia, all that remained of firm organization was the District of Sokols Abroad. To it now fell the task of upholding the Sokol idea and maintaining the Sokol tradition. Reconstituted in 1950 as the Czechoslovak Sokol Abroad, it now itself has five districts, one of them the Sokol Gymnastic Association of Canada, whose current president, Frederick Falta of Montreal, is also a vice-president of the international organization. Within this framework, further Canadian units were formed in Kitchener (1952) and Windsor (1953), another unit in Toronto, Sokol Toronto 2 (1953), Rouyn-Noranda (1955), and Ottawa (1960). The formation of the Sokol Toronto 2, a sequel of the already described cleavage in the Czechoslovak National Alliance between newcomers and old-timers, also signalled the beginnings of organizational divergences in the Sokol ranks. In 1955, a new roof organization was formed, the Canadian Sokol Organization, to which the Sokol Toronto and the units in Windsor and Batawa adhered. Its president is Frank

Janák, of Batawa, and it is patterned on the National American Sokol, which has always had an independent existence. The resulting split between the Sokol Gymnastic Association of Canada and Canadian Sokol Organization, regrettable in a movement which derives its strength from commonly held high ideals, is about to be healed. In January 1967, the two Sokol units in Toronto merged, assuming the name of Sokol Gymnastic Association of Toronto with a single president, Ervin Sypták. An independent Canadian Sokol organization is to be retained, but its units will be at liberty to affiliate themselves also with the Czechoslovak Sokol Abroad, and most probably will. In any case the international organization is already an important one, with something like 100,000 members the world over. Thus the Sokol idea, which did not die despite earlier persecutions of its followers, is certain to live also through the present vicissitudes.

The Canadian Sokols have themselves held five "slets," so far: in 1952 at Masaryktown in Toronto; in 1955 in Montreal; in 1960 in Noranda; in 1962 on the grounds of the Canadian National Exhibition in Toronto; and in 1967 on those of Expo '67. The last-named was at the same time the second "slet" of the Czechoslovak Sokol Abroad, attended by faithful members from all over the Free World. It was a memorable occasion, and a powerful demonstration of the undying Sokol spirit. How contagious it is is clear from the fact that in Canada, as indeed elsewhere, a number of members of the Sokol units are not even Czechs and Slovaks: the devoted chairman of the Rouyn-Noranda Sokol, Fred Pearson, is a native of London, England. Finally, it should be mentioned that a Czech Canadian from Toronto, John Waldauf, is the physical director of the world-wide Czechoslovak Sokol Abroad. He is, incidentally, also a member of Canada's National Advisory Council on Fitness and Amateur Sport.

Masaryk Memorial Hall Incorporated in Toronto, later renamed Masaryk Memorial Institute Incorporated, got its provincial letters patent in February 1945. A charitable endowment, it was started in life by 203 donors from the Czech and Slovak community who collected among themselves just under $16,000. In the list of founders we find men already encountered in these pages: Gustav Přístupa, Prokop Havlík, Joseph Chmel, Rudolph Koreň, John Mráček, Charles Buzek,

Mathew Pavlík. Broadly speaking, the aims of the Institute were twofold: to serve the cultural needs and well-being of the Czech and Slovak Canadians, and to strengthen the ties of Canadian-Czechoslovak friendship. Under present circumstances, work toward the second purpose must remain in abeyance; the first has been vigorously pursued for twenty-three years.

The scope of the Institute's activities is shown in the following listing of its principal departments: Masaryk Memorial Hall, Masaryktown Recreation Centre, the weekly newspaper *Nový Domov* ("New Homeland"), with connected bookshop and printing plant, the supplementary Czech and Slovak school, and the English-language courses, Masaryk Library, and the Circle of Dramatic Arts. Apart from these regular major tasks, all manner of other activities are supported, for example, the folklore group, Circle of Moravian Slovaks. The Institute has at different times offered a home to other organizations of the national group, the Sokol Toronto for instance.

Masaryk Hall is a year-round meeting place where conferences, dances, bazaars, amateur theatricals, and the like, are held. Masaryktown, in Toronto's suburban Scarborough, is a great patch of green, ideal for rest, amusement, and sport. The Czechoslovak Day, with a varied folklore and sports program, is held there every year on the first Sunday after Dominion Day. At the supplementary school, Czech and Slovak children, who otherwise frequent English-language schools, are given additional periods of instruction in the history and the language of their forefathers. This in good part is what is meant by maintaining the national cultural heritage. After many years of fruitful work under the chairmanship of Gustav Přístupa, and after him of Prokop Havlík and Frederick Čecha, the Masaryk Memorial Institute now has Ervin Sypták of Toronto as acting president, and Adalbert Škubal of Toronto as secretary-treasurer.

One of the groups which use Masaryk Hall extensively for its activities is the Women's Council of the Czechoslovak National Association, founded in the fall of 1960. It does much unobtrusive charitable work, especially for the Czech and Slovak refugees in camps in Germany, Austria and Italy, including the old, disabled, or sick, fated to remain there because they are ineligible for immigration. Newcomers to Canada are also given help and guidance. The members of the Women's Council pay no fees; each contributes as best she can in money, time, and talent. The president of the group, Ruth Petříček, is herself a woman of many parts. She has a Czech church family background—her father was Reverend Kamil Nagy, the last pre-war chairman of the Synodical Council of the Evangelical Church of the Czech Brethren—and is very active in Toronto religious life. The Women's Council's devoted work was recognized in 1964 by the *Chatelaine* Award for Service to the Community. It holds the yearly Czechoslovak bazaar in Masaryk Hall, and in another mundane but also most important sphere, it has contributed to the well-being of Czech and Slovak Canadians by the publication, in 1965, of a cookbook of national dishes.

The Czechoslovak Society of Arts and Sciences based in New York, does not strictly speaking belong in a Canadian book, but it deserves at least a mention. It has some one thousand members of standing in the scientific, literary, and artistic worlds, about 150 of whom are resident in Canada. In the west, Professor Moravčík of the University of Alberta acts in a liaison capacity for the society, while in eastern Canada this is done by a Czech-Canadian Toronto lawyer, Joseph Čermák, who is also the editor of the society's official bulletin, *Zprávy SVU* ("News of the Society of Arts and Sciences"). There is a Toronto chapter, as well, which has organized exhibitions of rare prints and of paintings by Czech and Slovak Canadian artists.

The veterans of the Czechoslovak legions which in the First World War fought on the Allied side in Russia, France, and Italy, used to be organized in the powerful Association of Czechoslovak Legionaries. It, too, was suppressed in Czechoslovakia after 1948 by the new communist regime, but lives on in exile in London, England. The Czech and Slovak Canadians who served in the two world wars are generally in Canadian veterans' organizations, the Navy League of Canada, the Royal Canadian Legion, and the Royal Canadian Air Force Association. In the Canadian Legion, there is even one Slovak, and one Czechoslovak, branch. The Slovak branch in Fort William, which has always had some Czech Canadian members as well, is the older of the two; it was chartered in November 1936, as the Canadian

Legion of the British Empire Service League, Canadian Slovak
Veterans Branch 129. It had fifteen charter members, all veterans of
the allied armies of the First World War, some still alive and stout
members of the branch. By two successive charters the name was
changed to the present one of the Slovak (Manitoba and North-West
Ontario No. 129) Branch of the Royal Canadian Legion. It is a very
active organization, with its own fine building, a Ladies' Auxiliary,
and close to three hundred regular members. The president is currently J. E. Adams.

The idea of a Czechoslovak branch of the legion in Toronto has
been mooted since 1952, but the group was accepted by the national
organization, and given its charter, only in 1962. Its official name is
the Czechoslovak Branch (Ontario No. 601) of the Royal Canadian
Legion. All through the years of preparation the driving spirit was
John Mráček, who is now the branch president. He, incidentally, is a
veteran of the Czechoslovak Legion in Italy of the First World War.

Although the overwhelming majority of Czech and Slovak war
veterans are, as we said, members of all-Canadian organizations,
there also exist small, separate groups. The Slovak Legion, originally
formed in Great Britain in 1950, also comprises men who served on
the Allied side in the Second World War. Understandably, it has for
some time been trying to gain incorporation in the Royal Canadian
Legion. In the meantime, it is affiliated with the Mutual Cooperation
League, a Toronto organization representing some east European
ethnic groups. Somewhat incongruously, there is also a Union of
Slovak Combatants, former servicemen who still seem loyal to the
memory of the armed forces of the German-allied Slovak State.

Ethnic newspapers, the good ones at any rate, have two principal
missions: to provide relatively recent immigrants who as yet cannot
read English or French with the usual information in periodicals; and
to apprise those who already read the English- or French-language
press of items of special ethnic interest. These are both worthy
objectives, and the ethnic press thus fulfils an important function in
Canadian life. After all, the over two million new immigrants who
have come to this country since the Second World War form a first
generation of new Canadians, many of whom remain dependent on

the ethnic papers for years. And in Canada as a whole well over five-and-a-half million people are of other origin than British or French, and are likely to remain interested in events in their national groups and in the preservation of their cultural heritages.

Even so, the Canadian ethnic press has always faced grave difficulties. The shoestring on which it operated may have become a little longer and stronger in recent years, but not by too much. In the majority of cases the editor is now fully employed by the paper and not forced as before to find his livelihood elsewhere and slave as an ethnic journalist at night. Still, he is as often as not a jack-of-all-trades; editor, writer, advertising manager, even printer's assistant. There was a time not so long ago when it was virtually impossible for an ethnic newspaper to get advertising. This is no longer so, and it has helped. Even today, however, ethnic publications depend heavily on the enthusiasm of publishers and occasional financial backers, often of modest means themselves, and of editorial staffs who work for meagre wages to provide an essential service for the national group. Conditions are, as we said, improving, and the ethnic press in Canada is consequently becoming materially stronger and thus more stable. For some years now it is joined in the Canada Ethnic Press Federation, whose current president is Charles Dojack (Dojáček), son of the familiar animator of Czech and Slovak activities in the Canadian west, Frank Dojáček.

The stringency under which the ethnic papers have always had to work has led to their affiliation with some wealthier organizations of the national groups. The experience of the Czech and Slovak periodicals in this country show how necessary this is. There have been twenty-seven different ones in the last fifty-eight years. Of these, less than half a dozen have managed to keep their heads above water for many years and can by now be considered reasonably secure: *Nový domov* ("New Homeland"), *Kanadský Slovák* ("Canadian Slovak"), *Slovenský hlas* ("Slovak Voice"), *Naše Hlasy* ("Our Voices"), *Ľudové zvesti* ("People's News"). They are the organs of, respectively, the Masaryk Memorial Institute, the Canadian Slovak League, the Canadian Slovak Benefit Society, the Czechoslovak National Association, and the Slovak Benefit Society of Canada.

We have briefly mentioned these and other papers earlier in the chapter. The very first Czech or Slovak periodical in Canada was the *Slovenské slovo* ("Slovak Word"), published in Blairmore, Alberta, as far back as 1910. With the total Slovak population (including a handful of Czechs) in the Crow's Nest Pass area then numbering only a few hundred, is was an over-ambitious enterprise sustained only by the unbounded enthusiasm of the editor, George Kleskeň, a printer from the Turiec region of Slovak Upper Hungary, and his backer, Andrew Lukča, a Slovak American from Chicago. Not surprisingly, the paper ceased to publish after about one year. Kleskeň tried again and again in later years to bring out a paper which, despite the unpromising environment and consequent lack of strong outside backing, would somehow become viable. His hopes were dashed each time, with the *Hlas národa* ("Voice of the Nation") which he launched in 1932, and the *Naša mládež* ("Our Youth") of 1937. Equally unsuccessful was a short-lived attempt in 1940 to revive the old "Slovak Word." George Kleskeň thus did not achieve much, but he deserves to be remembered as the first newspaperman in the Czech and Slovak community in Canada and a man of great heart.

The next two newspapers were started in Montreal, both in the same year, 1929. One was the *Slovenské bratstvo* ("Slovak Brotherhood"), which carried the subtitle, "Organ of Democratic Slovaks in Canada." After some changes in organization and direction it became the *Slovenský priekopník* ("Slovak Pioneer"). As such, and under the editorship of Stanislas Zúber who had come over from the *Hlas ľudu* ("Voice of the People") and the *Nová Vlasť* ("New Fatherland"), it got embroiled in an action for defamation that knocked the last prop out from under an already shaky financial structure and it ceased to publish in 1943. The other paper, *Kanadské noviny* ("Canadian Newspaper") entered life with much better chances, for it was at first owned by the well-established Czech New York periodical, *New Yorkský denník* ("New York Daily"). Written in Slovak and Czech, it was later published by a Slovak Canadian, George Kurdel. In 1942, it became the *Kanadský Slovák,* organ of the Canadian Slovak League. The *Canadian Slovak* at first remained in Montreal, then was published for seven years in Winnipeg, and in Toronto from 1959 onwards. Its first editor was Stephen Hreha, but ever since it moved to Toronto it has been guided by Dr. Frank Orlický. In the intervening years, the paper's editor for a while was the historiographer of the Slovaks in North America, Constantine Čulen.

Also well backed was the weekly *Nová vlast'* ("New Fatherland"), which started publication in Montreal in 1934. The Czechoslovak Benefit Society of Canada was behind it, as well as the Sokol units in Montreal and Toronto, and it also became the official organ of the big Slovak mutual benefit associations, the Western Society and the Eastern Society. At the outbreak of the war, under the able editorship of Martin Dudák, the "New Fatherland" got a further boost when it was made the organ of the powerful Czechoslovak National Alliance in Canada. Entirely devoted to the cause of Czech and Slovak unity, the paper was written in both languages. It subsequently shared the fortunes of the National Alliance. When evil days befell the latter for a time after the war, the "New Fatherland" stopped publication in 1948. The weekly *Naše hlasy* ("Our Voices"), published in Toronto since 1954, though independent, can now be considered the organ of the Czechoslovak National Association in Canada. Also written in both languages, it is a paper of high intellectual standards. Its editor is George Hlubuček, and the chairman of the editorial board, Joseph Čermák.

For almost twenty years now, the Masaryk Memorial Institute has published the weekly *Nový domov* ("New Homeland"); written in Czech and Slovak, it is also of high quality, as ethnic papers go. Its editor was for many years the experienced Prague newspaperman Rudolph Nekola; later it was his brother Charles, and now is Henry Zoder, who was previously very active in radio work. On the Institute's presses is also printed the journal of the Permanent Conference of Slovak Democratic Exiles in the United States and Canada, *Naše Snahy* ("Our Efforts"). It appears six times a year, and has attracted some of the best Slovak writers of Czechoslovak orientation on this continent.

The lineage of the present organ of the Canadian Slovak Benefit Society, the *Slovenský hlas* ("Slovak Voice"), goes back to 1934 and Bellevue, Alberta, where the old Western Society began to publish a small paper, *Úvahy* ("Deliberations"), soon renamed *Hlas národa* ("Voice of the Nation"). It, too, did not last long: as we have seen, the Western Society found it more convenient to make use of the Montreal "New Fatherland," as the Eastern Society was doing. After the merger of the two Slovak mutual benefit societies, the "Slovak Voice" was started in Windsor, Ontario, in 1949, at first as a monthly. Transferred to Toronto in 1951, it has now become a substantial weekly disseminating company information and providing all the other services of an ethnic newspaper.

We have already briefly mentioned the organ of the Slovak Benefit Society of Canada, and especially its vicissitudes at the beginning of the Second World War because of its pro-Communist leanings. The first paper the society published, beginning in the summer of 1931, was called *Naše slovo* ("Our Word"), and its editor at the start was Julius Húska. It became the *Robotnické slovo* ("Workers' Word") in 1932 and the *Hlas ľudu* ("Voice of the People") in 1936. It was under the latter name that it was suppressed by the authorities in 1940. The present weekly, *Ľudové zvesti* ("People's News"), has come out continuously since 1941.

Among the supporters of the Slovak State of 1939–45 who, after the latter went under with the defeat of Nazi Germany, came to Canada as refugees, there were many highly educated men who, naturally enough, wanted to make their opinions known here. They started a number of publications, all more or less short-lived: *Rozvoj v emigrácii* ("Development in Emigration"), in Montreal; *Náš život* ("Our Life"), which later became *Domovina* ("Homeland"), in Toronto; and even one which rather artlessly they called *Domobrana* ("Home Guard"), after the fascist-type militia of the Slovak State. They all foundered, because a steady diet of eastern European politics, especially old politics, does not attract many readers in Canada, and because the papers lacked the indispensable backing of an established ethnic organization.

All the Czech and Slovak papers, including those too weak to live or too esoteric in content to be read, have helped to maintain the ties within the ethnic communities. The great number of them seems to indicate considerable fragmentation in that community, but this is not really so. Of the five bigger periodicals now extant, the *Canadian Slovak* propounds the "independent Slovakia" line of the Canadian Slovak League; in three others the Czecho-Slovak theme is stressed: straightforwardly in "Our Voices" and "New Homeland" and with a Marxist variation in the "People's News"; the "Slovak Voice" has in recent years assumed a more or less uncommitted position. All of them are now largely oriented toward Canada, with "old country" affairs definitely taking second place. They adequately fulfil the general functions of Canadian ethnic papers, and even with Czech and Slovak immigration reduced to a trickle, they will remain important for as far into the future as one can foresee.

Bibliography

A GEM for the Canadian Mosaic, Masaryk Memorial Institute, Inc., Toronto, 1957.

Almanacs, Canadian Slovak Benefit Society, Toronto 1960, 1966.

Almanacs, Canadian Slovak League, Winnipeg, 1953–57; *ibid.*, Toronto, 1959, 1960, 1962.

Almanac, Slovak Evangelical Lutheran Church in the United States, for the year 1955, Pittsburgh, Pa.

Booklet of the Czech Mission House, Montreal, Christmas 1963.

BUZEK, KAREL *et al.*, *Památník Československé Kanady* ("Memorial of the Czechoslovak Canada"), Winnipeg, Oct. 1943.

By-laws, Masaryk Memorial Institute, Inc., Toronto.

"Český Bratr" ("Czech Brethren"), *Journal of the Evangelical Church*, 16, nos. 10–11 (Prague, Oct. 23, 1939).

GIBBON, JOHN MURRAY, *Canadian Mosaic: The Making of a Northern Nation*, Toronto, 1938.

—— *The new Canadian Loyalists*, Toronto, 1941.

KAYE, V. J., "Canadians of Slovak Origin: A Brief Survey," *Canadian Slavonic Papers*, 4 (1959).

KIRKCONNELL, WATSON, *Seven Pillars of Freedom* (2nd ed.), Toronto, 1952.

Naše Snahy ("Our Efforts"), *Journal of the Permanent Conference of the Slovak Democratic Exiles*, 2 (March-April 1965).

Notes on the Canadian Family Tree, Dept. of Citizenship and Immigration, Canadian Citizenship Branch, Ottawa, 1960.

Památník ("A Memorial"), of the 50 Years' Anniversary, Canadian Czechoslovak Benevolent Association, Winnipeg, Man., 1963.

Pamätnica ("A Memorial") to 25 Years' Anniversary, Canadian Slovak Benefit Society, Toronto, 1957.

Rekem, J., *Souvenir Book* (to the Fifth Anniversary of the Church of Visitation
      and to the Twentieth Anniversary of the Saint Michael's Catholic Slovak
      Society in Winnipeg), Winnipeg, Man., 1957.
"Slovenskí Jesuiti v Kanade" ("The Slovak Jesuits in Canada"), *Journal of the
      Slovak Jesuit Fathers, Galt, Ont.*; Toronto: St. Joseph Press, 1966.
Tlapák, Václav, "Národní a kulturní život krajanů v Kanadě," ("The national
      and cultural life of our countrymen in Canada"), *Naše Zahraničí*, Journal
      for the problems of emigration, 2 (Prague, 1931).
Vojta, Václav, *Czechoslovak Baptists*, Czechoslovak Baptist Convention in
      America and Canada, Minneapolis, 1941.

Czech and Slovak Canadian periodicals.

CHAPTER FOUR

The Czechs and Slovaks in
present-day Canadian life

We come now to the last part of our task: to describe the present contributions of the Czech and Slovak community to Canadian life. When
judging how the Czechs and Slovaks have been faring in Canada, one
must bear in mind that the fate of a national group in a new country is
seldom a matter of luck. Immigration is an investment. The newcomer brings himself, with a capital that consists in most cases only
of intangible values: his manual skills, his knowledge, the nimble-
ness of his mind, his will to work, his civic morale. The country of his
choice is the enterprise into which he puts himself and his capital
assets. If the investment is sound and the opportunities offered for
using it good, the immigrant and the country prosper. But if one or
other of the two essential ingredients is missing, the attempt at settlement fails. In other words, immigration is a two-way street: both the
immigrant and the country must give in order to receive.

This sounds pretty commonplace, but the fact is that this obvious
requirement is not always met. Many countries—Canada not excluded,
though blessedly things were changed early in the game—have looked
at the immigrant as an animated tool, to be bought for the price of
the passage, taken on inventory at the point of disembarkation, and
then shipped to wherever a cheap-to-maintain instrument of that kind
was needed. In the absence of any effort toward human management,

it was left to the immigrant alone to see how he could overcome all obstacles and find a niche in his new homeland. Proper settlement was entirely up to him. On the other hand, immigrants have been known to be ill-motivated towards their new country, to be demanding, and unprepared to give. Some are acting in bad faith; they consider the standard answer on the immigration form of why they wanted to come—"to settle"—a permissible white lie, and see their new country as merely a convenient place to lie over between two revolutions in the old country. Either way, the aim of immigration is missed.

Between Canada on one side and the Czech and Slovak immigrants on the other, there has generally been a good give-and-take relationship. Since settlement started in the rural west and only began to be significant around the turn of the century when there was already a firmly established and sound governmental policy for the development of the vast lands between the Ontario border and the Rockies, the Czech and Slovak newcomers found a smoothly working organization for their reception and a reasonable measure of practical assistance. The urban settlers, of course, fared less well. For a long time they were left largely to their own devices in an environment where every man had to fight for himself. Communal ties were tenuous. The Anglo-Saxon majority was the one that mattered, for Czech and Slovak settlement in Quebec Province was of no great account except in Montreal, and there, too, the tendency was to join the English-speaking part of the population. Though not unsympathetic toward the immigrants, this majority did not generally admit them into its midst. The Czechs and Slovaks, by nature no builders of ethnic ghettos, were compelled to rely on their own national organizations which were preciously few until the twenties of this century. Alternatively, they could lean, where possible, on the organizations of other Slavic groups. In the main, the rural Czech and Slovak immigrant of the earlier period found a hospitable "giving" country, whereas the urban had to suffer most of the difficulties besetting a poor man in a coldly foreign land.

Canada became the "giving" country *par excellence* in the Second World War and thereafter. Social legislation, interest in immigration

Ladislas Koldinský

Professor Vladimir Krajina

Walter Koerner

Adolph Velan

Leon Koerner

Rudolph Fraštacký

Thomas Bata and Mrs. Bata

spreading from government to the community, the crumbling of the walls of prejudice, general prosperity, all these factors combined to make it that. Still, the sensitive newcomer has perhaps only in recent years been spared that sense of isolation in a seemingly harsh, strange country which invariably assailed his predecessors. Fortunately, with the help available today, he can do much to avoid these feelings himself. A Czech writer who spent some time in Canada in the late forties and early fifties, Zdeněk Němeček, described this period of loneliness and dejection before the new country gives fully not only of its bounty but also of its soul, in a novel to which he gave the title of *Tvrdá země* ("A Hard Land"). It is a pity that he could not stay to see what a kindly one Canada really is.

All in all, then, Canada has done its part in the give-and-take exchange of immigration. For some it comes belatedly perhaps, but for that the more wholeheartedly. Let us see now how the Czech and Slovak immigrants have kept up their side of the bargain.

It seems hardly necessary to start off with the statement that the Czechs and Slovaks are civilized peoples, boasting a culture as ancient as any in western Europe. They were that long before the eighties of the last century when they first began to enter this country as settlers. The point here is not whether that culture manifested itself by this or that great achievement. What is significant when one is uprooted from the native environment and thrown into a completely foreign one, is the richness of the cultural heritage that has come down through the generations; in the end this is the main crutch on which the emigrant can lean. To show how rich this heritage of the Czechs and Slovaks is, and how many were the generations which built it up, here are two comparative examples. Charles University in Prague was founded in 1348, admittedly long after Oxford, but earlier than any such institution of higher learning in central and eastern Europe. The Acadamia Histropolitana, Bratislava University, founded in 1467, was also among Europe's first. The first book printed in Czech was published in Plzeň in 1468; the first printed in English, in Bruges in 1475. (It is interesting, and demonstrates the essential unity of development of western civilization, that the two printings were of the same book, *The Chronicle of the Trojan War*.) All in all, then, their cultural possessions handed down and augmented through the ages should be a very substantial asset to the Czechs and Slovaks, wherever they may find themselves in the world. They do have something of value to offer to their new countries. How much this will be in each case, will, of course, depend on the individual.

As already noted in Chapter Two, the first settlers in Canada from the national group were the Slovak farm labourers of the 1880s, who turned miners in the United States, and farmers again in the Canadian west. They suffered from all the handicaps which at that time fell to the lot of their people under Hungary, then still a feudal state ruled by the nationalist Magyar upper class. There were hardly any Slovak schools, and very little chance for a poor boy (and none at all for a poor girl) to progress beyond the elementary school level. Although no reliable data on this question exist for the years around 1880, the fact that even in 1910, according to official statistics, 26.8 per cent of all children in Slovak Upper Hungary were illiterate speaks eloquently for the conditions under which the Slovaks were condemned to live. Of their great cultural heritage these oppressed and neglected people could bring along only some traditional domestic skills and a little folklore and art. They were sturdy people, however, and as they gave willingly to their new country all they had, theirs, too, was in the end a successful immigration.

Except for some exceptional cases, the more notable in that they are so few, Canada received the full benefit of what Czech and Slovak culture and civilization had to offer only through the immigrants who came after 1918. It was then that the more perfect mutual exchange began between the newcomers, who brought in needed assets, and Canada, which gave them the opportunity to use these assets to best advantage.

The contribution that Czech and Slovak Canadians have made to the life of this country will be described under four headings: the arts, business and industry, scholarly pursuits, and various other activities. This is done only for convenience. An able man or woman is hardly ever successful in only one field; versatility is always a feature of intelligent people. In some cases it will be necessary to force an activity or a person rather arbitrarily into one of the four slots, and, of course, the scope of this book will preclude any attempt to be exhaustive. Only the significant and the typical will be dealt with and as what is significant or typical is a matter of judgment, unintentional errors of judgment and omissions will inevitably occur.

THE ARTS

The Czechs and Slovaks are artistic people. One expression of this fact is their national costumes, nowadays of course only adornments for festive occasions, which show an inbred sense of colour and style. Their artistic nature is evident in the beauty of their handicraft and in the quantitative and qualitative richness of their folk rhythms. Music has in fact always permeated Czech and Slovak life. The "šumař," the untaught musician who instinctively reaches for his cheap little violin to play the tune which has just crossed his mind, is as characteristic of this national group as the southern Italian who at any moment will give out with an operatic aria is of his people. These are seeming stereotypes, but they are true enough to life. The love of making music, as distinct from the mere love of music, has been preserved in Czechoslovakia even in these days of radio and gramophone and spreading artistic non-participation.

At the time when Czech and Slovak mass immigration to Canada started, Czech music was at its height of accomplishment and world renown. The great old masters, Smetana, Dvořák and Fibich, were dead, but they had set a tradition and a style. Smetana's opera, *The Bartered Bride*, has always enjoyed international popularity. His majestic symphonic poem, *My Country*, and the patriotic festival opera, *Libuše*, had filled the hearts of a nation with pride in history and country and with hope for the future. Dvořák's chamber music, his *Slavonic Dances*, the oratorio *Stabat Mater*, his symphonies, above all the Fifth, "From the New World," became if anything better known abroad than Smetana's work. Fibich is the least appreciated internationally of the three, but his influence at home almost equalled Smetana's and Dvořák's. Apart from other pieces, he set to music the great Czech poet Jaroslav Vrchlický's dramatic trilogy, *Hippodamia*.

Smetana, Dvořák, and Fibich were followed by a whole bevy of later composers of high stature, such as Foerster, Ostrčil, Kovařovič, Janáček, whose work already reaches into the period of Czech and Slovak settlement in Canada that interests us here. Janáček was perhaps the first to open the road to modern music and a new tonality. At least one of his eight operas, *Jenufa*, has been performed the world over. And hard on the heels of this middle group of composers came a great number of modern ones, such as Martinů, Křička, Jeremiáš, Weinberger, Hába, and then Axman, Kvapil, Nejedlý, to name but a few.

As for Slovak music, apart from the folk music which has a richness and a lilt all of its own, Miloš Francisci and J. L. Bella were the first to achieve prominence, the latter particularly through his opera, *Wieland the Blacksmith*. M. Schneider-Trnavský, and after the last war, Eugene Suchoň with his operas *Krútňava* and *Svätopluk*, and Alexander Moyzes with his "Tatra" symphonies, became widely known well beyond the borders of their homeland.

The performing side was at an equally high level. Here, in particular, it is possible to mention only a very few names, for outstanding musicians abounded in Czechoslovakia. The opera ensembles of the National Theatres in Prague and Bratislava maintained throughout a high standard of excellence. They were restocked with talent developed in the permanent opera companies which were a quite common feature of Czechoslovak provincial towns. The Czech Philharmonic Orchestra under Wenceslas Talich enjoyed world renown, and so did the Czech (or Bohemian) Quartet of Hofmann, Suk, Nedbal, and Wihan, two of whose members, Joseph Suk and Oscar Nedbal, were also important composers. From among the virtuosos, Kubelík, Kocián, Firkušný became perhaps best known abroad.

This cursory outline of the state of the musical art in Czechoslovakia has been given to show the greatness of the musical tradition and the proficiency which the Czech and Slovak immigrants brought to Canada. If ever one can speak of the cultural enrichment of a country through immigration, one can in this case.

Czech and Slovak musicians first presented themselves to the Canadian public at the beginning of the Second World War. Within the Montreal Branch of the Czechoslovak National Alliance a musical "team" performing varied compositions assembled whose members were Sonja Pečmanová, Oscar Morawetz, Walter Schmolka, and Frank Stein. With the express aim of popularizing Czechoslovak music, the group gave the first of its many concerts in Montreal in March 1941. A special performance, of Dvořák's works only, was given in commemoration of the master's hundredth birthday on February 12, 1942. In the fall of that year a trans-Canada tour was undertaken, which took the group as far west as Victoria, British Columbia. The four originals also did yeoman work on the CBC's Czechoslovak half-hour, for a long time a regular program. Frank Stein, incidentally, still teaches music in Montreal. Sonja Pečmanová is with the Montreal Symphony. Walter Schmolka, too, continues to be an active musician; he has also for many years headed the Czechoslovak section of the CBC's short-wave International Program. Of Oscar Morawetz, who grew to be one of Canada's leading composers, we shall say more later on.

Another concert group was formed in Toronto by the late Dr. Francis Pokorný. It was named Emmy Destinová Quartet after Dr. Pokorný's famous aunt, perhaps Czechoslovakia's greatest female operatic singer. In Toronto, also, there has been active for years the Circle of Moravian Slovaks, which we mentioned already in Chapter Three in connection with the Masaryk Memorial Institute. It specializes in folklore music, dances, and dramatics. Similar groups, which keep alive the knowledge and appreciation of Czech and Slovak folk songs, are active in a number of other organizations of the national group.

The performing musician from Czechoslovakia with the longest standing in this country is the Slovak-Canadian organist of the Church of Saints Cyril and Method in Montreal, O. M. Sinčák. He has worked here in church music since 1934. A professor of music at the University of Montreal, he also holds a diploma from the University of Chicago and one of Gregorian singing awarded him by the Thomas More Institute, and he is still an active choir-master and singer. In Chapter Three we have noted that some of the Czech and Slovak churches in Canada have outstanding choirs. These are invariably due to the devoted work of the musically gifted people so numerous in the national group. To give one typical instance from among many, there is Dr.

Joseph Kyselka, the fine organist and founder and director of the choir at Saint Wenceslas' Church in Toronto.

Czech and Slovak Canadians are nowadays found everywhere in the expanding musical life of this country. Thus the jazz-composer George Traxler, once immensely popular in Czechoslovakia, wrote some of his best pieces later on in Montreal. Others may have brought their musical souls from the old country, but have already received their musical training in Canada. Again we can only mention one of these younger musicians as a characteristic example. In 1935, Helen Hájnik came as a very young girl, from Czechoslovakia to Assiniboia. Blessed with a fine mezzo-soprano voice, she received vocal instruction in Regina, and in Peterborough and Toronto, Ontario. Since then she has appeared in numerous CBC recitals and operas performed on television, and has also been active in the musical education field.

The best-known Czech-Canadian singer is undoubtedly Jan Rubeš —in fact, he is probably the most widely known male singer in Canada. A graduate of the Prague Conservatory and already enjoying a background of success in Europe, he came to Canada shortly after the communist coup in 1948. Endowed with an engaging personality and unbounded stamina, he gained popularity almost overnight. Jan Rubeš has appeared in leading operatic roles at the Stratford and the Vancouver festivals and with the New York City Opera; he has sung at concerts, and been for years star and host of regular television ("Rhapsody") and radio ("Songs of My People") programs. Perhaps more than anybody else, he has popularized Czechoslovak music in this country.

Among the Slovak Canadian performers, the outstanding figure is the violinist Charles Dobiáš. He, too, is one of those who got their musical education in this country, in which he arrived as a boy of eight in 1932. A pupil of Kathleen Parlow at the Royal Conservatory of Music in Toronto, he was still finishing his formal studies when he was appointed concertmaster of the Canadian Opera Company. From there he went, again as concertmaster and later assistant conductor, to the National Ballet Company of Canada. These days, he is the first violinist of the Toronto Symphony, a member of the Toronto String Quartet, and soloist and concertmaster of the Pro Arte Orchestra. He performs in the National Festival Orchestra, the Chamber Music Workshop at the Stratford Festival, and frequently on CBC television and radio. At forty-four, Charles Dobiáš is now reaching the height of a remarkable career.

Conductors from Czechoslovakia have been the leading animators of musical activities throughout Canada. Thus, Hans Gruber, in the years that he led the Victoria Symphony Orchestra, did a great deal to develop young Canadian talent. Nicholas Goldschmidt, who came to Canada in 1946, was the musical director of the Opera Festival Company of Toronto, later the Canada Opera Company, from its inception, and then, starting in 1958, artistic and managing director of the Vancouver International Festival. More recently, he has guided the development of cultural programs for the 1967 Festival Canada. He has also taught music, and is a much sought guest conductor in Canada and abroad. A more recent arrival, Vladimír Jelínek, is with the Quebec Ballet, and has also conducted at Expo '67.

Walter Susskind, a native of Prague and an alumnus of the State Conservatory of that city, was on a European concert tour when the tragedy of Munich occurred. He remained in England, worked there throughout the war, and after it became a veritable musical citizen of the world, through which he has taken his conductor's baton in seemingly incessant travels. An outstanding piano virtuoso and a conductor of world renown, he is also a prolific composer. In this latter field, he has ranged from string quartets and song cycles to operas and film scores. Many of these compositions clearly show Walter Susskind's cultural background, for instance his often performed "Nine Slovak Sketches." His travels brought him to this country for the first time in November 1955. At that time he was the conductor of the Victoria Symphony Orchestra in Melbourne, Australia and the next year he moved to Canada permanently. As successor to Sir Ernest MacMillan, he was for ten years the conductor of the Toronto Symphony. After giving up this position to Seiji Ozawa, he turned his main energies to his own creation, the National Youth Orchestra, which he led to its first overseas tour in the fall of 1966. Today, after twelve exceptionally productive years in this country, Walter Susskind is a leading figure in the musical world of Canada.

When Oscar Morawetz joined the musical "team" mentioned earlier which was organized by the Montreal branch of the Czechoslovak National Alliance, he was twenty-three and had just arrived in Canada. Born in Bohemia, in Světlá nad Sázavou, the son of Richard Morawetz, who was a friend of Thomas Garrigue Masaryk and later, in Canada, an indefatigable worker for Czechoslovak causes, he studied music in Prague. In Canada, he attracted attention with his first of many orchestral compositions, "Carnival Ouverture." From then on, his career as a composer has followed a steadily ascending curve. He is the holder of many awards, Canadian and international, a highly acclaimed piano virtuoso, a Doctor of Music, and professor of music of the University of Toronto. That he has been called by the critics "the most performed composer in Canada" is perhaps the best assessment of his standing in the musical world. As Oscar Morawetz has lived his whole life in a family environment which takes great pride in the Czechoslovak heritage, he is archetypal of the good immigrant in a multi-cultural country.

A literary heritage is not as easily transferrable into a new environment as is a musical. Particularly difficult is the interchange between the Slavic languages and the Romance and Germanic. The spirit and flavour of a work is as often as not lost in translation. Thus, to give one example, the Czech post-1918 classic, *The Good Soldier Shveik*, though exceptionally well translated, falls almost flat in English. For a Czech or Slovak writer, the transition to working in English is extremely difficult, and to French perhaps only a little easier. In either instance, having written professionally in Czech or Slovak is very often a handicap rather than a help. As a rule, it is a matter of learning all over again how to express one's thoughts.

No wonder, then, that Czech and Slovak letters are all but unknown in the English-speaking world. Some plays by Karel Čapek, Jaroslav Hašek's *Schveik*, the odd modern novel by Egon Hostovský or Ladislas Mňačko (whose recent *Taste of Power* made something of a splash), a rare poetic work like Mácha's *May*, and some politico-historical writings like those of Thomas Garrigue Masaryk and Edward Beneš, is just about all available to the average English-language reader. Translations into French are a little more numerous, and there are even some works of Czech-Canadian writers—Pavel Javor, for instance, and Rudolph Nekola. Even so, it amounts to just a glimpse, and a very fleeting one at that, of the riches of Czech and Slovak literatures.

The great majority of the Czech and Slovak writers who came to this country continued to write in their native languages. The wonder is that they keep on writing at all, considering how unrewarding the task is. Czech and Slovak readership on this continent is small, publishing facilities are limited, and the works of writers living in exile (and into this category fall all those who left Czechoslovakia to escape communism) are still banned in Czechoslovakia where the great mass of the potential readers are. Some years ago, Joseph Čermák, himself one of the undaunted band of Czech and Slovak writers in this country, put it this way: "Czech and Slovak writers would be well advised to throw their tools into the garbage and get themselves jobs as carpenters. Strangely enough, though perhaps not so strangely, this is not what happens. Czech and Slovak letters in Canada are flourishing and the number of people engaged in this pursuit is rather impressive." Čermák, incidentally, makes his living otherwise than as a writer, but not as a carpenter. He is a busy lawyer in Toronto.

Perhaps because it is very difficult to get anything in Czech or Slovak published in Canada, slim volumes of poetry see the light more often than heftier volumes of fiction. Probably the first of these books of verse, published in Montreal in April 1943, was Rudolph Nekola's *Noc v hoře Královské* ("The Night in the King's Mountain"). The author, then a captain in the Czechoslovak army-in-exile, had just come to Canada on a recruiting mission—he later came back to stay—and his first impressions of the immense, wintry country were strong. He saw all of it, from Halifax, where his ship docked, to Quebec, where he spent his first Canadian Christmas, to Vancouver, and he tells about it engagingly in some of the twenty-seven poems in the little volume. Among Rudolph Nekola's later work there is also a novelette, *Cariocký chodec* ("The Carioca Walker").

The most prolific and best-known of the Czech poets in Canada is Pavel Javor. This is the pen-name of George Škvor, a professor of Slavic literatures at the University of Montreal and editor of the

Czechoslovak section of the International Service of the CBC. A native of Martinice near Prague and a Doctor of Law of Prague University, he gained his PhD. in this country. No fewer than nine collections of his lyrical verse have been published in quick succession since the first came out in Toronto in 1953, under the title, *Daleký hlas* ("Voice from Far Away"). One, *Kouř z Ithaky* ("Fumes from Ithaca"), published in New York, has been called "the chief poetic event in 1960" in the field of Slavic letters on this continent. As his later offerings show, Pavel Javor is still growing in depth of perception, sensitivity, and sheer technical skill. The gentle sadness which permeates his work also comes out strongly in his first Canadian novel, *Kus života těžkého* ("A Hard Portion of Life"), serialized in the Toronto publication, "New Homeland" and more recently published in book form. With some of his poems translated into English, French, German, and Russian, Javor has acquired a name far beyond the Czech and Slovak community in Canada.

Joseph Čermák has published a selection of poems, *Pokorné návraty* ("Humble Returns"). He has also written in English. His *God and Men* and *This Lonely Earth* have been honoured with University of Toronto Epstein Awards. Zdeněk Rutar wrote *Doma a za mořem* ("At Home and Beyond the Seas"). Another Czech novelist is Jaroslav Havelka (*Pelyněk*, "Hemlock") who incidentally, is a distinguished professor of psychology at the University of Western Ontario.

From among the numerous Slovak Canadian practitioners of *belles lettres* we already mentioned O. M. Debnárkin, with reference to his work as a newspaper editor. He is also a lyrical poet, with a published collection of verse, *Zjavným hlasom* ("With an Emphatic Voice") to his credit. In it, he makes the point that it is the language of one's fathers which gives to the immigrant the inspiration he needs to live contentedly in his new homeland. This in fact, put in Debnárkin's poetic language, is the *leitmotif* of Canadian immigration policy, successful integration through the maintenance of the ethnic cultural heritage and, ensuing from this, group identity. More turned toward the past, to the lost Slovak homeland, is the work of another Slovak lyrical poet, Cyril Ondruč, whose verse appeared under the eloquent title *Pahreba* ("Ashes").

The religious theme is stressed in the two collections of poems by the Reverend J. Dragoš-Alžbetinčan, *Nepoškvrená víťazí* ("Immaculata's Victory") and *Slávme hviezdy jasné* ("Let us Celebrate the Clear Stars"), the latter including a moving hymn to Saints Cyril and Method. L'udo Bešeňovský, Jožo Zvonár-Tieň and John Doránský are other poets popular in the national group. Zvonár-Tieň also wrote a versified drama *Ohne* ("The Fires"), and Doránsky a play, *Stará mať neopúšťaj nás* ("Grandmother Do Not Leave Us"), which was successfully staged by amateur companies in this country. Miloslav Zlámal, who has done also a good deal of politico-military writing, has published two collections of verse, *Exil* ("Exile") and *Keby se jaro nevrátilo* ("If Spring Did not Return").

Among Slovak Canadian writers of non-fiction, Reverend John Rekem and Dr. Joseph Kirschbaum stand out. The former wrote a book of memoirs, *Trenčianska Vážnica*, but otherwise he is essentially an important literary critic and philologist who specializes in Slovak literature of the seventeenth and eighteenth centuries. In this field, he has written monographs on "Štefan Dubničay, 1675–1725," the Slovak historian and polemist, and on *Slovak Literature and National Consciousness before Anton Bernolák, 1762–1813*. He is also the author of the instructive *The Origin and Development of the Slovak Language*.

Joseph Kirschbaum, too, has worked in the field of literary history. His publications include, in chronological order of the subject matter *Literature of the Cyrillo-Methodian Period and Slovakia, Anton Bernolák, the First Codifier of the Slovak Language, Pavel J. Šafárik, L'udovít Štúr and his Place in the Slavic World*, and *Pan-Slavism in Slovak Literature*. As can be seen, Kirschbaum ranges through the whole of the old and middle periods of Slovak literature, to the second half of the nineteenth century. Essentially, though, Joseph Kirschbaum is a politico-historical polemist. A former secretary-general of Hlinka's Slovak People's party and one of the leading lights of the Second World War Slovak State, his aim is to explain that political structure, and in view of its link with the Axis, perhaps to justify it in North American eyes. In this vein are written his *Náš boj o samostatnosť* ("Our Fight for Independence") published in the United States, and *Slovakia's Struggle for Independence*, published in this country.

It is rather difficult to decide whether or not one should count the late Constantine Čulen as a Slovak-Canadian writer. He had a Canadian period, during which he was also editor of the "Canadian Slovak" and he wrote a monograph, *Slovaks in Slovakia and Canada*. His principal work is, however, in the wider sphere of his people's settlement in North America. Here, he published before the war his *Slováci v Amerike* ("The Slovaks in America"), and then, in the days of the Slovak State, the definitive work, *Dejiny Slovákov v Amerike* ("History of the Slovaks in America").

Czech-Canadian political and politico-historical writers have generally not gone—or perhaps not been able to go—beyond contributing articles to the periodicals of the national group. This goes even for those who like Ota Hora, a former deputy in the Czechoslovak parliament, were in the old country prolific authors with several published books to their credit. Transplanted into the Canadian environment, they may have had a good deal to say still, but did not find the material conditions for saying it in print. One of the few exceptions is the author of *The Battle of Home*, Anthony Cekota, who wrote under the name of Václav Hanák. Originally a native of Moravian Napajedla, he has lived in Canada since 1939. This book, published during the war, describes how eighty of the 40,000 employees of the giant Bata concern got out of occupied Czechoslovakia to found the Canadian factory and settlement at Batawa, Ontario, and how they fared in the new environment. This is the core of the book, which also deals with wider issues of industrialization and its influence on man's future. Anthony Cekota's later writings have been concerned with the relationship between automation and education.

Henry Zoder has published an account of the Prague revolution of May 1945, *Pražská revoluce* ("The Prague Revolution"). He also wrote a historical drama, in English, *King Wenceslas*, which was produced in Toronto by the Central Stage.

A special breed are the Czech and Slovak Canadian writers who have completely immersed themselves in the Canadian literary world and are thus, purely and simply, English-language authors. The best-known in this group, Peter Newman, cannot rightly be considered influenced in his work by his ethnic background. He was born and raised in Moravian Břeclav, but he came to Canada as a young boy and got his education at Upper Canada College and the University of Toronto. Peter Newman is a widely read columnist of the *Toronto Daily Star*, and the author of best-selling books, including the brilliant if controversial biography of John Diefenbaker, *Renegade in Power*.

By contrast, George Gross, sports writer of the *Toronto Telegram*, and especially Lubor Zink, Ottawa columnist of the same paper, are essentially Czechoslovak journalists transplanted into Canada, now writing exclusively in English, and dealing with their subject matter from a Canadian point of view. Zink has become something of a Canadian Cato whose "cæterum censeo" is the insistent warning against weakness toward communism. A poet and novelist in the old country, Zink has had two books published in Canada in English, *The Uprooted*, and *Under the Mushroom Cloud*, the latter a selection of editorials he wrote when with the Brandon, Manitoba, *Sun* between 1958 and 1961. Into the same category with George Gross and Lubor Zink belongs one of the authors of this book, editor of the monthly *Commentator*, and frequent contributor to the Toronto *Globe and Mail* and Canadian periodicals. In vastly different fields, the Jelíneks, world figure skating champions of 1962 about whom we will hear more later on in this chapter, have written their life story; and F. J. Bernard has published a text-book, *Dynamic Displays*, which has recently appeared in a fourth edition. With the Czech- and Slovak-Canadian scholars who also publish their work in English we will deal later in this chapter.

In general, Czech and Slovak painting and sculpture have proved as little adaptable to exportation as Czech and Slovak literature. This is again because, up to most recent times, when the new art forms have internationalized them as it were, they were so much bound up in the domestic milieu, which was colourful and typical enough to satisfy the artists. Not that the artists did not go abroad. A good many did, and especially in Paris there was always a sizable Czech artists' colony, to which have belonged some of the greatest Czech painters, Wenceslas Brožík, for instance, Luděk Marold, Alfons Mucha, and Francis Kupka. But even their work remained for the most part characteristically Czech and thus not always easily understandable to a world public. There were, of course, exceptions—Marold, who was immensely popular in France, was one—but they only prove the rule. It may be mentioned in passing, that Brožík should have become famous on this continent, curiously enough, for his painting "Columbus at the Court of Isabelle", which was reproduced on the United States five-cent stamp in the 1893 Columbian issue; but nobody knew or cared who the artist was.

What can be said about the nineteenth century masters, Joseph Mánes and Mikoláš Aleš, for instance, is also true of the leading twentieth-century modern Czech landscape painters like Anthony Chitussi or Julius Mařák, the impressionist Anthony Slavíček, the portrait painters of the stature of the Czech Max Švabinský and the Slovak Janko Alexy, and the many excellent engravers and delicate book illustrators. Only in recent times have Czechoslovak artists of advanced genre and techniques, George Trnka for example, acquired a following commensurate with their international renown.

The most typically Czech and Slovak school of painting found its subjects in the colours and graceful movements of an idealized country scene. Understandably, the painters of this genre have come mainly from those parts of Slovakia and from the Moravian-Slovakian borderland where the national costumes are the most striking. Joža Úprka, a Moravian, not only set a style but also inspired a large group of Slovak artists on the other side of the old Hungarian border. How close the relationship was of the painters on either side of the Little Carpathians is shown by the fact that the Slovaks of the beginning of the century used to exhibit their work on the Moravian side, in Hodonín. The earliest, in 1902, was Jozef Hanula, who put into his paintings all the melancholy of the pre-1914 Slovak lands. In 1907, the livelier impressionist Gustav Mallý appeared on the scene. Later, in Czechoslovakia, Martin Benka became the leader of the folklore school, with a number of talented followers, like Miloš Bazovský and Janko Alexy. These artists can be fully appreciated only in their homeland; their art may be enjoyed outside Czechoslovakia, but it is not transplantable.

The same strongly national characteristics are apparent in Czech and Slovak sculpture. The great Joseph Myslbek, whose statue of Saint Wenceslas on Prague's square of that name has been called "the epitome of the nation's spirit," set the tone. Some of the later sculptors, men like John Štursa and Otakar Španiel, did, however, find a closer link with the mainstreams of world art than most of the Czech and Slovak painters ever did.

All this had to be said to explain why more of the Czech and Slovak painters and sculptors now abroad have not managed to gain recognition. Especially those from the folklore schools, or those strongly influenced by the Czechoslovak milieu, have brought with them a wellnigh insuperable handicap.

Still, a number of Czech and Slovak Canadian artists have found deserved success. Jaroslav Šejnoha, a diplomat-turned-artist, who at the time of the communist take-over in Prague was Czechoslovak ambassador to India, is now a member of the Canadian Academy of Arts; his works have been widely exhibited in Canada. There is the many-talented John Zach, painter, sculptor, engraver. There are graphic artists like Sonja Waldstein, and delicate ceramics designers like Zdeněk Vykoukal. There is Anthony Lněnička, a painter who has also done a good deal of stage designing. There are other active painters, Mathew Kousal, Klement Olšanský, J. Celestýn, to name a few. Among them, Anka Majer also has become fairly well known beyond the frontiers of Canada. A pupil of the eminent German expressionist Oscar Kokoschka, she has exhibited in South America, Spain, and Italy. The work of Father Lang, SJ, as a painter, sculptor, and art teacher we have already mentioned. The painter John Koerner has been teaching at the Vancouver School of Art.

In the performing arts, and particularly the theatre, the obstacles in the way of an actor or an actress projected into a completely different language environment from his or her own are particularly formidable. Some Czechs and Slovaks have overcome them, but in Canada there are no Voskovecs, Haases, or Štěpáneks. No Czech or Slovak Canadian has made the big-time English- or French-language stage. The closest has perhaps been Milada Třešňák-Redly, who played the leading female part in the New Canadian Theatre production of Mika Waltari's *The Witch Will Return*. A Czech Canadian, Mike Janeček, has, incidentally, taken a leading part in the organization and direction of this interesting Toronto theatre group, composed of players from a great many ethnic communities. Devoted mainly to presenting to the Canadian public the works of lesser-known non-Anglo-Saxon authors, the New Canadian Theatre made its debut in 1963.

There have been and are a good many Czech and Slovak amateur theatre groups which perform in the native language. They generally form in conjunction with one of the national halls, and are sustained by the devoted and unselfish work of a few enthusiastic individuals who receive little outside recognition. Here, we can mention only one of these groups, as an example characteristic of most others. The Circle of Dramatic Arts at the Masaryk Memorial Institute has through the years staged a whole string of important plays. The standard of performance has been high. For a decade this was in a large measure the work of Rose Hais, who under her stage name of Růžena Karičová had been a well-known actress in Czechoslovakia and who was director and often manager of the Circle's performances.

The architects and the builder-architects are perhaps also best dealt with in this section, even though in some cases the technical is understandably of more account than the artistic. We have already mentioned some of them in Chapter Three—men like Andrew Midlík, Steve Sura and Frank Štalmach, who have designed many important public and private buildings in this country. To these may be added such as George Pokorný, who, after getting his degree at the Prague Polytechnic, came to Canada in 1928 and has worked here ever since with great success; and Rudolph Papánek, who was among the leading designers of Expo '67. In a rather different field, Joseph Kalenda is chief designer with Canadian National Railways.

Outstanding in their field have been two men, the Czech Canadian Charles Rybka and the Slovak Canadian Gejza Horánsky. Their stories deserve to be told in some detail because they so strongly support the thesis (to which we must come back again and again) that to be successful, immigration must be a wholehearted and fair exchange between newcomer and country, both equally ready to give. Dr. Charles Rybka, born of Czech parents in Vienna and a graduate of Prague Polytechnic, came to Canada in 1928. It took him seven years to become the head of the Toronto office of a big Canadian firm of consulting engineers, and another eleven to establish his own company. Among the latter's more important projects have been, in Toronto, the Trinity College quadrangle and chapel, the Bell Telephone Company administration building, and the Lord Simcoe Hotel. He has worked on several structures at Waterloo University and on hospitals all over Ontario. Dr. Rybka holds a number of patents and has written many technical papers. He now teaches the young of his profession by lecturing at the Ryerson Polytechnic Institute in Toronto. All in all, Dr. Rybka's is the kind of life story one would want to tell in the publicity pamphlet of an immigration office.

Gejza Horánsky, who died in Montreal in August 1966, came from Vel'ká Bytča in Slovakia. Before the war he was mainly a builder of modern highways, anything but an easy task in his mountainous native land. Emphatically opposed to the fascistic Slovak State, he joined the Slovak National Uprising of 1944. His practical contribution was the rapid adaptation to heavy military traffic of the patriots' only airfield, Tri Duby, near Banská Bystrica. He was working on a second emergency field, on the Muráň plateau, when the uprising was crushed by the Germans and their quisling helpers. Horánsky went into hiding, and survived to see the day of liberation. But three years later, after the Communist coup, he had to flee from his homeland, after all. He worked for a while in Holland and in Morocco, and then came to Canada. In the McNamara Construction Company, which he joined here, he quickly worked himself up, through sheer competence, to a top position on the engineering staff. There can be no better proof of how good he was than that he was entrusted with a key job in the building of the Montreal subway, le Métro. He drove the project forward with unflagging energy in order that it be completed by the time Expo '67 opened. In the process he drove himself to a heart attack and death at the age of sixty-two. Gejza Horánsky was the complete immigrant, if ever there was one. He was a faithful member of the Czech and Slovak group, active especially in the Permanent Conference of Slovak Democratic Exiles. To his new Canadian homeland he gave everything he had, in the end his life.

BUSINESS AND INDUSTRY

Czechoslovakia had been born, on October 28, 1918, with a silver spoon in the mouth. Bohemia and Moravia together constituted the economically most developed part of the Austro-Hungarian Empire, accounting between themselves for no less than 52 per cent of its total industrial output. Slovakia was much less advanced, of course, but relatively—that is, compared with the general economic backwardness of the Hungarian part of the old Dual Monarchy—still not too badly off. It had some industry, though no heavy one, and a number of operating mines. In one field at least, the production of cellulose, Slovakia was actually in first place in central Europe. Agricultural production was on a high level, though not uniformly so, in both the Czech and the Slovak parts of the young Republic.

There thus existed a basis for economic progress, excellent in Bohemia and Moravia, somewhat tenuous but capable of development in Slovakia. In fact, all hopes entertained in 1918 were amply fulfilled. Czechoslovakia advanced rapidly until 1929, weathered the Great Depression better than any other country of eastern and central Europe, and from 1935 onwards was on a rapid upswing again until the German occupation put an end to it all. This was achieved by hard work, thrift, and individual enterprise in a free market economy, and by the judicious economic policies of successive governments. An American economist of German extraction who had watched the spectacular growth of the Czechoslovak economy from close quarters, Gerhard Schacher, put it this way:

Here was a country of hard-working people leading a modest life, strictly limited by the framework of its current earnings, thus increasing its national fortune without foreign help and saving a considerable part of its annual income. Here was a country and a nation that knew it had to depend mainly on its own economic possibilities and the expansion of its trade, and not at all on foreign loans and political gifts. There was no other country in Central Europe which was to such a degree able and willing to modernize and rationalize its entire economic system by its own means and almost entirely without foreign support. That this was done in Czechoslovakia without aiming at self-sufficiency was one of the greatest economic achievements in Central Europe after the World War.

These same enterprising businessmen and industrialists, who had been largely responsible for Czechoslovakia's economic success, became the targets of persecution during the war-time German occupation and especially after the Communist take-over in 1948. There never was a free market economy in Czechoslovakia after Munich. After an initial purge on racial and national grounds, the economy was tightly controlled and directed by the occupying power in the Protectorate Bohemia-Moravia, and by the autocratic, Axis-oriented state in Slovakia. Then came a short period of somewhat circumscribed democracy entailing widespread nationalization. This was in turn supplanted by complete collectivization under the post-1948 Communist government. From 1938 onwards, then, a Czech or Slovak desirous of building his future at home by dint of his own enterprise had no longer any real opportunities.

Many of these men made their way to Canada, started here again from the beginning, and again made good. As always, the instances we will give of Czechs and Slovaks who founded important businesses and industries, to their benefit and to that of Canada, are merely meant as examples. In choosing them, we did not have any firm criterion. Size, international importance, particular interest to Canada, novelty, all were taken into consideration. No attempt has been made to enumerate the biggest enterprises established by Czech and Slovak Canadians, for this would have meant deviating from the purpose of this book.

When one speaks of Czechoslovak industries, the first name to come to mind usually is Bata. Thomas Baťa, Sr., started with a small hand manufacture of slippers, which he built up until, at his death in an aircraft accident some years before the Second World War, he owned the biggest shoe concern in the world, with headquarters in Zlín, Czechoslovakia. The home factories were lost, but the Bata Shoe Organization today is larger than ever. It is directed from Toronto by the founder's son, Thomas Jr., and consists of a roof organization, Bata Limited, and of eighty-seven independent Bata companies in eighty-four countries. Headquarters, through Bata International Centre in suburban Don Mills, provides the whole global network of establishments with research and development, consulting, and managerial services and, when necessary, with financial support. All in all, the giant concern employs about 71,000 people the world over and produces something like a quarter of a billion pairs of shoes a year.

The beginnings of the present organization were modest, indeed.

We have already referred to them briefly in this chapter in connection with Anthony Cekota's book *The Struggle of Home*. The attempt almost did not come off. The eighty or so experts from Zlín, with their families, were ashore in Quebec City, but the all-important machinery, some eight hundred crates, was on board a German freighter which docked in Montreal around September 1, 1939, and then made off downstream again without discharging its cargo—the captain rightly estimated that Canada's entry into the war was imminent and he wanted to avoid internment. The RCMP gave chase, but, Canada being still formally at peace with Germany, could only persuade the skipper to unload, after all. This they did successfully—one of the unsung, diplomatic triumphs of the Mounties—and the Batamen got the tools of their trade. A shoe factory, an engineering works, and a factory settlement, Batawa, Ontario, were quickly built. The latter, consisting now of close to two hundred homes and about eight hundred inhabitants, has, incidentally, the distinction of never having needed a communal police force. There has been no serious crime in Batawa in all the twenty-eight years of its existence. This is no doubt due to the unusual group coherence in this factory settlement, which has no fewer than eighteen different cultural and sporting associations and social clubs.

There are now three Bata shoe plants in Canada; together with the engineering works and the string of retail stores they employ about 2,500 people. This Canadian establishment is now the heart of what in the truest sense of the word is an industrial "empire." Batawa is no Zlín, but the wheel of which it is the hub is bigger than the old one was. Thomas J. Bata continues to preside over the concern, in which many of the top workers are still old-time Czech and Slovak employees from pre-war days.

The four Koerner brothers, who came to Canada in 1939, were of the third generation of a family who had gone into the lumber business around the middle of the nineteenth century and before the war owned the J. Koerner Lumber Industries Limited in Prague. They originally came from Moravian Hodonín, birthplace of the first president of Czechoslovakia, Thomas Garrigue Masaryk, who was a family friend. In Canada they started by buying a derelict lumber mill at

Dr. Anna Sirek   Dr. Otakar Sirek

Charles Dobíaš

Walter Susskind

Oskar Morawetz

Pavel Javor (George John Škvor)

Below: Jan Rubeš

Czech and Slovak Canadian dancers in national costumes

New Westminster, British Columbia. There, initially with about forty-five men, they started to saw western hemlock, which nobody wanted because it was considered unsuitable for industrial purposes. By a special treatment, the Koerners made it suitable—and removed the stigma unjustly attached to it by renaming it Alaska pine. A whole industry based on this material developed, led by the Koerners' own Alaska Pine Company. That hemlock was made into a marketable material turned out to be a great boon to British Columbia.

By the mid-fifties, the Alaska Pine Company was up among the giants of the British Columbia forest industry. It then ranked first in the production of pulp for textiles; second as a producer of lumber; fourth in wood pulp for paper and newsprint. Thus the two surviving Koerner brothers, Leon and Walter, had built themselves an industrial empire such as they could not have dreamed of in Czechoslovakia. Canada had been good to them.

They, in turn, have been good to Canada. With their business ambitions more than satisfied, Leon and Walter Koerner turned their energies more and more to public service and to philanthropy. It would be impossible to enumerate here all that the Koerners have done for worthy individuals, for Vancouver, the province, and especially for the University of British Columbia. The "Leon and Thea Koerner Foundation," established in 1955 with an initial endowment of one million dollars, made grants in the next ten years of over $750,000 to various projects in the fields of science, education, and the arts. Leon Koerner also donated the Faculty Club Building, and the Thea Koerner House which is the university's graduate students' centre, apart from providing money for a wide range of other causes. Walter has given large sums for the establishment of a department of Slavonic Studies at the University of British Columbia, and has generously supported the university library and the hospital. All in all, the Koerners' contributions now run into the millions of dollars.

Walter Koerner's public service, on the Economic Council of Canada and the Canadian Welfare Council for instance, has been recognized by the award of the Medal of Service of the Order of Canada, of which he is among the first fifty-five recipients, and so far the only Canadian of Czechoslovak origin so honoured.

In their operations, Bata and the Koerners have been representative of what is called, often pejoratively, "big business," but they have done it in a style free of some of the less engaging aspects occasionally associated with that type of enterprise. Thus, both Bata and Alaska Pine have always been distinguished by a high degree of social sense, and especially by good labour relations. Back in Czechoslovakia, the Bata concern already had a scheme of employees' participation in profits. Though fully organized by two international unions known for their toughness when it comes to protecting the interests of their members, the Bata shoe factories in Canada have yet to have a serious labour dispute, let alone a strike. And the Koerners' relations with their labour force were so good and so friendly that in 1946, at the height of a bitter International Woodworkers of America strike against the industry, Leon was the guest of honour at a dinner of the workers' bowling club. This, too, can be put down to the credit of these big Czechoslovak industrialists transplanted to Canada.

A kind of Horatio Alger story is that of Stephen Roman, a farm boy from Veľký Ruskov in Eastern Slovakia, who came to Canada in 1937, when he was not quite seventeen. Today he is at the head of a Canadian uranium empire, with subsidiary enterprises producing cement in Ontario, bread in the United States, phosphates in Peru, gold and platinum elsewhere in South America, and copper in Ireland.

Roman started out in business in 1946, with $5,000, unbounded energy, and above all a lot of imagination. His first venture was the Concord Mining Syndicate, which engaged in exploration for base metals and oil. Then, in 1953, he went into the Blind River country and uranium ore mining. An old copper-and-nickel firm, North Denison Mines, served as a basic corporate structure. Around it, Roman formed his two present big companies, Consolidated Denison Mines Limited and Can-Met Exploration Limited. Large-scale development began around Elliot and Quirke Lakes. Tens of millions of dollars were poured into the operations themselves, into communications, and into the building of company settlements. The combined capacity of the uranium concentrators of the two companies is now around 12,000 tons a day.

The country lad who became a financial magnate is a man of many parts. He is a breeder of prize cattle at his Romandale Farm. Slovak causes in Canada, though not Czech and Slovak, have in him their most generous supporter. For instance, he was largely instrumental in organizing the Cyrillo-Methodian celebrations of 1963, to mark the eleven hundredth anniversary of the arrival at Rostislav's court of the Slav Apostles who brought Christianity to the Great Moravian State. The Holy See has bestowed high honours upon Stephen Roman in recognition of his work as a leading Roman Catholic layman. His closest business collaborator is another Slovak Canadian, John Puhky.

In the old country, Rudolph Fraštacký, native of Mošovce in Slovakia, had been active in the field, highly developed before the war, of agricultural co-operatives. In the days of the Slovak State, he worked in the underground and had a hand in the Slovak Uprising. Then, from 1945 until 1948, he was a member of the Council of Plenipotentiaries, the *de facto* cabinet of autonomous Slovakia. Because of his work, there, and as one of the leaders of the Slovak Democratic party, he was a marked man, and in fact only escaped by the skin of his teeth. In 1949 he arrived in Canada. An exceptionally energetic and able man, Rudolph Fraštacký was soon successful in a variety of interconnected business enterprises, the importation of steel products, lumber manufacture and lumber dealing, building, land development, advice and assistance to foreign investors. In 1962, he founded in Toronto the Metropolitan Trust Company, of which he has ever since been the president. Under his guidance, the total moneys administered by the company have grown sixfold in five years, from about twenty-five million dollars at the end of 1962 to some hundred and fifty million dollars at the end of 1967. At the same time, Rudolph Fraštacký has throughout the years taken a very active, indeed a leading, part in the work of the Czech and Slovak community. Again, in his case, we see this most desirable combination of adherence to one's own national heritage and of hard-working loyalty to Canada.

Ninety-five per cent of the vessels of the United States Navy are equipped with steam traps invented and manufactured by a Czech Canadian mechanical engineer, Charles Velan. Valves developed and produced by him are used in some fifty countries of the free world in chemical processing and rocketry, in oil refineries, and nuclear reactors. Once again, the story of Charles Velan is that of a man who came to Canada with no other capital than the knowledge he carried in his head, found the right environment here, and used it to the utmost, for his own benefit and that of the country.

He was born and raised in Moravia, from birth in Moravská Ostrava to the gaining of a degree in mechanical engineering at the Brno Polytechnic, in 1939. Immediately after the war, amid very unfavourable conditions in Czechoslovakia, he formed his first company, and he has been his own boss ever since. When his enterprises were nationalized after the communist coup, he left the country. In 1949, Charles Velan arrived in Canada. The beginnings were difficult, but in 1953 he got his big chance with the first substantial United States Navy contract. Today, Velan Engineering Limited has two plants in Montreal, and subsidiaries in Plattsburg, New York; Leicester, England; and Nassau, Bahamas. Charles Velan is the holder of a number of important patents. He has presented several technical papers, especially in the nuclear field and in astronautics. These particular interests are expressed in his membership in the American Rocket Society and the British Interplanetary Society. As was the case with the Koerners, who also re-established a lost Czechoslovak business in this country, Charles Velan also only found in Canada the necessary elbow-room for the full development of his talents.

Our two final examples are perhaps on a lesser scale than the preceding, but for that more typical of what quite a number of hard-working and able Czech and Canadian entrepreneurs have achieved in this country. They may thus stand for all those not dealt with in this book.

Ladislas Koldinský had, since 1930, run his own fruit-processing plant in Heřmanův Městec, in Bohemia; his wife Libuše helped him as a research scientist. Their particular field was the extraction of pectin from apples, for use in jellies, jams, and marmalades. The Koldinskýs, too, were dispossessed by the communists and came to Canada in 1949. In Kentville, Nova Scotia, they found an enterprise, Canada

Foods Limited, which since the war had been largely inactive. Ladislas Koldinský, who in 1950 was appointed general manager of its fruit division, and a fellow Czech, Vladimir Fejtek, who took over the pickle division, combined forces to make the firm again into a prospering enterprise. They very soon succeeded and thereby provided a convenient market for the apple growers of the Annapolis Valley. Their crop today is not even sufficient, and Canada Foods imports fruit heavily from other parts of Canada. Similarly, its pickle division largely buys up the vegetables grown in the region. Under Koldinský's and Fejtek's direction, the firm has also built up a healthy export business. Expansion has been greatly helped by the technical and scientific advances achieved by the Koldinskýs, who in this country have further perfected their process of manufacture of pectin, and, in a different sphere, that of carrageen, the seaweed used in medicine as a demulcent. Ladislas Koldinský has now retired from Canada Foods Ltd., but Vladimir Fejtek continues their successful work in Kentville.

The great love of Jožo Weider, a native of Žilina in Slovakia, was always the mountains, especially in winter. Although he was a graduate in commerce, he preferred to run a modest tourist chalet amid the peaks not far from his home town. In Canada, where he arrived in 1939, he also made his living for some years as a ski instructor. After a good deal of moving from place to place he landed in Collingwood, Ontario. There, the idea came to him to build a big ski resort, which he called Blue Mountain Winter Park. For over a quarter of a century now, Weider has patiently assembled acreage, cleared slopes, installed tows, erected buildings. He has thus created the foremost resort of the kind in Ontario, and at the same time contributed more than anybody else to the popularization of skiing in the province. It is a sport now enjoyed by tens of thousands in Ontario, whereas at the time when Jožo Weider started to lay the physical foundations for it, there was just a handful of enthusiasts.

Weider branched out into industry more or less by accident. Among the Czech and Slovak Canadians he always liked to employ at the Collingwood resort was also Dennis Tupý, who in the old country had been a potter. Nobody paid any attention to the clay of the area except when it stuck unpleasantly to the boots after a rain, but Tupý did. He recognized it as good ceramic material, and he told Weider who thereupon established the Blue Mountain Pottery Limited. It has grown into a major regional industry; its fine products, many still with the flavour of the Czech and Slovak domestic art, are widely sold in Canada and exported abroad; and the company's showrooms not only serve their normal purpose, but are also a local tourist attraction.

If the half dozen, or so, examples we have listed prove anything, then, surely, it is that immigration of the right kind is a blessing to a country. The emphasis should be firmly placed on the qualifier, "of the right kind." The old policies aimed in the main at attracting willing—and cheap—manual labour are today totally obsolete. Not that a labourer should not be admitted. Common justice, humanity, sometimes self-interest, often demand that he should be. The point is, though, that he can only offer his own work. The man who can see a stand of hemlock or test a bit of clay between his fingers and then build an industry on his observations, gives work to hundreds and thousands and prosperity to a whole region. This, to a degree not often realized in this country, is the kind of immigrant Canada has frequently been getting from Czechoslovakia.

Many of the original enterprises have spawned others, in a continuous process of development. This is particularly true of Bata, where a good many of the experts who came in 1939 acquired in this country a taste for independent operation and set themselves up in business. Former Batamen have done this in Toronto and elsewhere in Ontario, in Hamilton, Burlington, Midland, Stirling. And these are not small factories, either. The Burlington and Hamilton plants, for instance, which belong to the same owners (Anthony Ronza and Vladimir Sedlbauer) employ about 425 people and produce a respectable 7,000 pairs of shoes a day. Where before the war there was only the occasional factory belonging to a Czech or Slovak Canadian—Stephen Rudinský's Montreal wire works, for instance—and even by 1943 a mere thirty-eight most of which were quite small, there is now hardly any branch of business and industry in Canada where there are no Czech- and Slovak-Canadian enterprises. This in turn has made the life of the members of the whole group quite a bit easier: there is usually employment to be found with a former countryman. Some of the firms have, in fact, made a point of giving work to recent immigrants from Czechoslovakia. It is a pity that there are so few of the latter, nowadays, to avail themselves of this opportunity, and ultimately, when they have found their feet in the country, of the wider opportunities Canada offers.

SCHOLARLY PURSUITS

In Czechoslovakia, the concept of the university was that of a seat of learning rather than, as it is here, the last stage in the educational cycle of any reasonably gifted young man or woman. Consequently, the professors in Czechoslovakia essentially were not teachers but scholars who read papers to a roomful of people who, characteristically, were not called students but listeners ("posluchači"). This system was, of course, not entirely inflexible. The seminar and the laboratory were places where the professors did teach. The polytechnic institutes were closer to schools in their manner of instruction. In general, however, the listener was supposed to be sufficiently developed to avail himself with little guidance of what the university had to offer. The generally tough major examinations for which he sat were the only tests of his progress, for there was hardly any assigned work, and none at all on some faculties. It was more or less up to him how he wanted to spend his university years, whether profitably or unprofitably.

It is debatable whether this ancient system, in which the professors are resident scholars and the students really paying guests, is a good one. Essentially, it catered to the élite. The universities were few and small: in Czechoslovakia, there were only three and two polytechnics of university status for ten-and-a-half million Czechs and Slovaks (and lesser Slavic minorities). There were also comparatively few professors, and their standard of scholarship was correspondingly high. They had a good deal of time for their own research, much more than the average member of a Canadian faculty has. In sum, the Czechoslovak universities were great seats of learning, but it took some individual effort to learn in their sacred halls.

Canada has received a number of men and women brought up in this system, somewhat crusty with age, but demanding and thus productive of often outstanding scholars. A typical example of this kind of scholarship is Dr. Vladimir Krajina, professor of botany at the University of British Columbia, where he has been teaching for close to twenty years now. A 1927 graduate of Charles University, he started his academic career at his alma mater. During the war, he became one of the leaders of the Resistance. As such, he was prevailed upon after the liberation to stay on in politics. This he reluctantly did, serving in the parliament of Czechoslovakia's short-lived democratic period, from 1945 to early 1948, with distinction and a courage very much needed at that time and place, while continuing to lecture at the university. The Communist coup then drove him into exile. In Canada, Professor Krajina has worked mainly in the field of plant ecology, where his research has contributed substantially to our understanding of how to preserve natural environment, and especially the forests. His studies have also taken Professor Krajina to the Canadian Arctic. He has been one of this country's delegates at the 1966 Pacific Science Conference in Tokyo. Apart from other activities, he is the editor of the University of British Columbia's yearly publication, *Ecology of Western North America*, and with a student group is working on a definitive study, "Vegetation and Its Environment in British Columbia." As a man who has been successful both in his old homeland and in his new, Professor Krajina has found his niche—a roomy one in his case—in this country without trouble and feels perfectly comfortable in it; but he also maintains an active connection with the Czech and Slovak Canadian community.

An interesting husband-and-wife team, Otakar and Anne Šírek, teach at the University of Toronto. They have always worked together, from the time in 1946 they both graduated *sub auspiciis*—with first-class honours—at the Komenský University in Bratislava and received their doctorates of medicine. They were together on a post-graduate scholarship in Stockholm, Sweden, when the Communists took over. The Šíreks thereupon went to Canada, where in 1950 they joined the staff of the Banting and Best Department of Medical

Research of the University of Toronto. Under Dr. C. H. Best, they worked in diabetes research, received their PhDs, and are now both associate professors in the university's Department of Physiology. On their respective merits, but in recognition of work done in common, the Šíreks are members of a number of international learned societies. They have also written extensively in their field in several languages, including Slovak when they started out on their joint scientific career, and English in more recent years.

Today, there are Czech and Slovak Canadians on the faculties of most universities in this country. It would be quite impossible to list them all. Just to give some examples, there are the historians Stanley Pech at the department of Slavonic Studies, University of British Columbia; Wenceslas Mudroch and Jaroslav Bouček at Carleton University, Ottawa; Reverend Anselm Spacey at the University of Ottawa. Head of the Department of Political Studies at Queen's University, Kingston, is John Meisel, whose published work includes a voluminous and minute analysis, *The Canadian General Election of 1957*. The same subject is taught by Richard Gregor at the University of Toronto and Bohuslav Kymlička at the University of Western Ontario in London. At the various schools of medicine, there are Jaroslav Havelka, whom we have already mentioned as a novelist, at the University of Western Ontario; Robert Weil at Dalhousie University in Halifax; Stanley Skoryna at McGill University in Montreal; Zdeněk Mézl at the University of Montreal. In other disciplines of the humanities, George Kolaja teaches sociology at McMaster University in Hamilton, Frank Uhlíř, the same subject and anthropology at Dalhousie; Dušan Břeský, modern languages at the University of Alberta; Reverend August Rakús, theology at St. Michael's College, Toronto. In the sciences, there are the mathematicians George Liška at the University of Saskatchewan, and Henry Lowig at Alberta, while George Lasker works at the University of Manitoba in the specialized field of advanced computer science. To round out the list, Ambrose Žitňák is an agronomist at the University of Guelph, Ivo Moravčík a professor of economy at the University of Alberta. Also working in the field of theoretical economics, though not in the academic one, is

Michael Ferik, who is with the Department of Economics of the Province of Ontario.

Not all the Czech and Slovak Canadians do their work at the universities. Nowadays, after all, much of research, even basic research, is done in the industrial laboratories. One of these retiring backroom boys, anonymous except in their narrow professional circle, is Dr. O. S. Pokorný, who has contributed greatly to the economic development of Canada. He retired a few years ago after a lifetime of service with the research department of Imperial Oil Limited in Sarnia, Ontario. Graduated with a doctorate in chemistry from Charles University in Prague in 1924, he came to Canada two years later with the intention of studying the pulp and paper industry, a field in which he then wished to specialize in Czechoslovakia. Fate brought him to Sarnia and the Imperial Oil laboratories, which were at that time in a somewhat embryonic state. Dr. Pokorný was interested, and stayed to serve there as a leading research scientist from 1928 to the end of 1964. During this time he saw the tiny department grow into a large and important scientific institution and he greatly contributed to this development. Lubricating oils were his specialty. As it is patently impossible to enumerate all the new processes and improvements of older ones for which he was responsible, one example will have to stand for the rest. As explained in the *Esso Reporter*, the company's house paper, "Dr. Pokorný played a key role in the design and development of the phenol extraction process for extracting impurities from lubricating oils. This resulted in engine oils with greatly improved resistance to oxidation. First installed at Sarnia, phenol extraction was later adopted world-wide and is still an essential part of lubricating oil processing."

Like every gifted man, Dr. Pokorný has always also had interests other than the purely professional. He has built high-fidelity sets and is an outstanding photographer; he has done, and in retirement is still doing, important community work in Sarnia, where he has led the campaign for the new Sarnia Public Library and has founded the Dramatic League, now the Sarnia Little Theatre. And through all his years in Canada he has remained attached to the national group from which he comes.

VARIOUS OTHER ACTIVITIES

Here, in this kind of final grab-bag, the various kinds of activity are so many that they defy thorough treatment. We must be very selective and limit ourselves to the more typical cases and to those showing a contribution of real significance to Canadian life.

To break into Canadian politics is difficult for one foreign born, both psychologically and materially. Much as he tries to immerse himself into the political problems of his new homeland, they seldom absorb him entirely. Almost always, in the back of his mind, there remain the old issues. Thus, for the authors of this book, Munich and the resulting destruction of Czechoslovakia is the traumatic political experience of their lives, not the Great Depression as it is for the majority of their Canadian contemporaries. This can become important when the time arrives to weigh the relative importance of domestic social as against foreign policy problems. For the group aged forty or so, who came to Canada after the communist coup, it is this event which sticks in their mind. This may be a minor inhibiting factor for a Czech or Slovak Canadian who would enter politics here, but it is one just the same. On the practical side, the system under which the riding association is ultimately the one which picks the candidate, at the provincial and federal levels at any rate, tends to work against the newcomer who, as it were, has not "been around" long enough to have much of a chance for a nomination. This, of course, does not affect the immigrant of at least second generation. A. B. Weselak, for instance, whose parents came from what is now Czechoslovakia but who himself was born in Beausejour, Manitoba, represented the Springfield constituency of his home province in the federal parliament from 1953 to 1957. He is now a member of the Immigration Appeal Board. On the other hand, George Ben, though born a Slovak, has been able to rise in Ontario politics. A former alderman of the City of Toronto, he was elected Member of the Provincial Parliament for Bracondale, and in the last election, for Toronto-Humber.

In the field of community service the name of Lotta Hitschmanová is a byword. She was the first secretary of the Ottawa branch of the Czechoslovak National Alliance at its formation in 1942, and in subsequent years did a great deal for Czechoslovak causes. As the long-time Executive Director of the Unitarian Service Committee of Canada she has been organizing assistance for the needy in many parts of the globe. In a very different field, Velen Fanderlík has been very active in the Boy Scouts movement in British Columbia. A former lawyer in Brno, Czechoslovakia, now teaching classics at Trail, British Columbia, he used to be the leader of scouting in his homeland.

It is difficult to determine all that should be included under the heading of aesthetics, or aesthetic pleasures. Perhaps gourmet cooking should. It is a Czech and Slovak forte, even though the products are probably as little exportable as some of the national art. Goethe, at least, called Bohemia the land of the Phaeacans, after the Lotus-eaters of *The Odyssey*, and he had cooking definitely in mind. Naturally, then, restaurants featuring the Czech and Slovak kitchen abound in Canada. A number of big Canadian establishments have Czech or Slovak chefs. One of them, Stephen Vojtech, was, for instance, chosen to prepare the state banquet in Ottawa for the Queen and Prince Philip on the occasion of their visit in 1957. Also in the field of aesthetics is the achievement of Eva Koclík, a young Toronto beauty queen, who represented Canada at the 1967 Teen International Pageant in Hollywood.

The contribution of Czech and Slovak Canadians to sports in this country has been outstanding. In figure skating, they have given Canada, in Maria and Otto Jelínek, the 1962 world pairs' champions. On their way up, the brother-and-sister team won the Canadian Junior, the Canadian Senior, and the North American Senior titles, and were once third in the world competition. The Jelíneks are now professional performers with the Ice Capades. In the same discipline, another brother-and-sister act, Svata and Mirek Staroba, have had great successes, and Jarmila Pachl was a Canadian women's figure-skating champion.

Ice hockey was made a spectator sport in Czechoslovakia only after Mike Buckna, a Slovak Canadian, went over from this country to Prague, some years before the war, to be a player, a coach, a developer of young talent. He laid the groundwork from which ice hockey, next to soccer, has grown to be the most popular sport in

Czechoslovakia. One of the little boys who batted a makeshift puck around on a frozen river with a tree branch is now one of the half dozen best players in the world, Stan Mikita. Adopted by his uncle and aunt, Joe and Annie Mikita of St. Catharines, Ontario, he came to Canada in 1948. In St. Catharines, he played with another Slovak Canadian youngster, Elmer Vaško, who also later became a famous National Hockey League player with Chicago and Minnesota. Mikita, of course, is the all-star centre of the Chicago Black Hawks.

In skiing, the three Weider girls, daughters of Collingwood's Jožo Weider, have won a good many races, including the Junior Canadian Ski Championships. Zdeněk Metzl, a student at the University of Montreal, has made a name for himself as a ski jumper.

In lawn tennis, Hana Sládek, incidentally the grand-daughter of Czechoslovakia's greatest pre-war all-round athlete, Karel Koželuh, was a Canadian women's champion. In table tennis, Max Marinko, a veritable indestructible, held the Canadian men's title for many years.

Mike Eben, of the University of Toronto Blues, a native of Žatec in Bohemia, was named Canada's best college football player for 1967, and as such was awarded the Hec Crighton Memorial Trophy. Significantly, Eben is also an excellent scholar, an honour language student at his university. Among the more esoteric sports, Vladimir Kavan is the co-founder of the Canada Balloon Club, and has himself participated successfully in a number of races. Unbelievable feats of sheer stamina, which at the same time broke all known Canadian records, were performed some years ago by Robert Mendl, who walked non-stop from Toronto to Chatham, Ontario and back, some 360 miles; and then from Montreal via Toronto to Chatham, 540 miles in 174½ hours—that's more than a week of marching on the road.

About the Sokol we have already spoken in a previous chapter. The Canadian units contain some male and female gymnasts who have excelled in competition. We would specifically mention one, Jerry Kasanda, as an example, both because of his personal performance and because of his contribution to physical fitness in the Canadian Armed Forces. Jerry Kasanda comes from southern Bohemia. He has been a Sokol since the age of five. A student at Charles University in

Prague at the time of the coup, he fled and came to Canada in 1949. After roughing it for three years as a farm labourer in Ontario, a lumberman in the North country, a ranchhand in Alberta, he enlisted as a private in the Princess Patricia's Canadian Light Infantry. From 1955, he was continuously employed as a physical fitness instructor. Commissioned at the beginning of 1963, Jerry Kasanda is now a captain, second-in-command of the physical education and recreation section at the big Canadian forces base, Camp Borden, Ontario. Captain Kasanda has also done a great deal of organizational work in his specialty in the forces, and he is, of course, still an active Sokol, as far as his comparative isolation permits.

Finally, there are the unsung men and women in the background who encourage and materially support amateur sports. One of these is Ladislas Myslivec, successful Toronto industrialist, a true friend of sports and Czech- and Slovak-Canadian sportsmen. Others have freely and unselfishly devoted their efforts and time to counsel and instruct young sports enthusiasts. Rudolph Piovaty, who represented Czechoslovakia in swimming at the Paris Olympics back in 1924, has done that, for example, around Brantford, Ontario. There are others, and more are coming up. Thus, among the newest arrivals in Canada, recently escaped from Czechoslovakia and a refugee camp in Austria, is the former coach of the Dutch and of the Czechoslovak national women's volley-ball teams, M. Puhlovský, one of the greatest experts on the game in Europe.

The men and women mentioned in this section are individuals who have made a name for themselves by their achievements. Needless to say, they are not the only Czechs and Slovaks who have made a contribution to Canadian life. The Saskatchewan wheat farmer, perhaps the fourth generation of a Czech or Slovak immigrant family which settled there, the fruit grower in the Niagara Peninsula, the foreman in an automobile plant, the small businessman on the city corner, have all—inconspicuously but effectively—made such contributions. There are only some 80,000 Czech and Slovak Canadians, about four-tenths of one per cent of the total population of Canada. This would be very little, were it not for the fact that the overwhelming majority have made a resounding success of settlement in this country, which is just about ideal for immigration. They all wanted to come. The prosperity and contentment of most of them prove that they have chosen well. And Canada has been enriched by their coming.

Bibliography

Archives of the Czechoslovak National Alliance in Canada, care of *Nový Domov*, Toronto.

BOUSCAREU, ANTHONY T., *International Migrations since 1945*, New York, 1963.

CEKOTA, ANTHONY, *The Battle of Home*, Toronto, 1944.

DRUCE, GERALD, *In the Heart of Europe*, London, 1936.

Encyclopedia Canadiana, vol. V, Ottawa, 1958.

Esso Reporter, Imperial Oil Ltd., Toronto (Feb. 1965).

GIBBON, JOHN MURRAY, *The New Canadian Loyalists*, Toronto, 1941.

HORÁK, BOHUSLAV (ed.), *Yearbook of the Czechoslovak Republic*, Prague, 1929.

KIRKCONNELL, WATSON, *Canadians All*, issued by the Director of Public Information under authority of the Minister of National War Services, Ottawa, June 1941.

PORTER, JOHN, *The Vertical Mosaic: An Analysis of Social Class and Power in Canada*, Toronto, 1965.

PORTER, MCKENZIE, "Leon Koerner's One-Man Giveaway Program," *Maclean's Magazine*, 69 (Aug. 4, 1956).

RECHCÍGLE, MILOSLAV, JR. (ed.), *The Czechoslovak Contribution to World Culture*, The Hague, London, Paris, 1964.

Slavs in Canada, Inter-University Committee on Canadian Slavs, Edmonton, 1966.

SMREK, JÁN (ed.), *Slovenská Prítomnost' Literárna a Umelecká* ("The Slovak Literary and Artistic Presence"), Prague, 1931.

Fortune, "The Biggest—and Best—Speculator in Canada" (Sept. 1966), 67.

WAGNER, VLADIMÍR, *Profil Slovenského Výtvarného Umenia* ("The Profile of Slovak Creative Art"), Turčiansky Sv. Martin, 1935.

Czech and Slovak Canadian periodicals.

Index

PERSONS AND INSTITUTIONS

PLACES